24.95

Primary Source Accounts of the
Spanish-
American War

KENNETH E. HENDRICKSON, JR.

MyReportLinks.com Books

an imprint of

 Enslow Publishers, Inc.

Box 398, 40 Industrial Road
Berkeley Heights, NJ 07922
USA

MyReportLinks.com Books, an imprint of Enslow Publishers, Inc. MyReportLinks®
is a registered trademark of Enslow Publishers, Inc.

Library of Congress Cataloging-in-Publication Data

Hendrickson, Kenneth E.
  Primary source accounts of the Spanish-American War / Kenneth E. Hendrickson, Jr.
    p. cm. — (America's wars through primary sources)
  Includes bibliographical references and index.
  ISBN 1-59845-007-7
  1. Spanish-American War, 1898—Sources—Juvenile literature. I. Title. II. Series.
  E715.H475 2006
  016.9738'9—dc22

                         2005031169

Printed in the United States of America

10 9 8 7 6 5 4 3 2 1

To Our Readers:
Through the purchase of this book, you and your library gain access to the Report Links that specifically back up this book.
The Publisher will provide access to the Report Links that back up this book and will keep these Report Links up to date on **www.myreportlinks.com** for five years from the book's first publication date.
We have done our best to make sure all Internet addresses in this book were active and appropriate when we went to press. However, the author and the Publisher have no control over, and assume no liability for, the material available on those Internet sites or on other Web sites they may link to.
The usage of the MyReportLinks.com Books Web site is subject to the terms and conditions stated on the Usage Policy Statement on **www.myreportlinks.com.**
A password may be required to access the Report Links that back up this book. The password is found on the bottom of page 4 of this book.
Any comments or suggestions can be sent by e-mail to comments@myreportlinks.com or to the address on the back cover.

Photo Credits: Avalon Project, Yale Law School, p. 102; Duke University, p. 88; Enslow Publishers, Inc., pp. 8, 76; Grolier Multimedia Encyclopedia, p. 70; Historical Museum of South Florida, p. 53; Illinois State Military Museum, p. 55; Library of Congress, pp. 3, 10, 12, 13, 15, 33, 35, 40, 42, 44, 46, 57, 61, 63, 66, 72, 80, 84, 98, 104, 107, 112, 114; MyReportLinks.com Books, p. 4; National Archives and Records Administration, pp. 19, 22, 100; National Archives and Records Administration/United States Department of Defense, pp. 1, 51, 59, 74, 106; National Museum of Health and Medicine, p. 62; National Park Service, p. 93; New York Public Library, p. 86; Ohio State University, p. 25; PBS, pp. 37, 68; Smithsonian Institution, National Museum of American History, p. 90; Smithsonian Institution, National Portrait Gallery, p. 32; The Spanish-American War Centennial Web Site, p. 92; The Theodore Roosevelt Association, p. 28; United States Army Center of Military History, pp. 81, 84, 95; United States Military Academy, p. 49; United States Navy, Naval Historical Center, p. 23; University of Northern Iowa, p. 78; University of South Florida, p. 29; University of Wisconsin, p. 18; Veterans Museum and Memorial Center, p. 113; White House Commission on Remembrance, p. 110.

Cover Photo: American soldiers in the trenches, the Philippines, c. 1898; National Archives and Records Administration/United States Department of Defense.

Every effort has been made to locate all copyright holders of material used in this book. If any errors or omissions have occurred, please contact us at www.myreportlinks.com. We will try to make corrections in future editions.

CONTENTS

MyReportLinks.com Books
Great Books, Great Links, Great for Research!

The Internet sites featured in this book can save you hours of research time. These Internet sites—we call them **"Report Links"**—are constantly changing, but we keep them up to date on our Web site.

When you see this "Approved Web Site" logo, you will know that we are directing you to a great Internet site that will help you with your research.

Give it a try! Type http://www.myreportlinks.com into your browser, click on the series title and enter the password, then click on the book title, and scroll down to the Report Links listed for this book.

The Report Links will bring you to great source documents, photographs, and illustrations. MyReportLinks.com Books save you time, feature Report Links that are kept up to date, and make report writing easier than ever! A complete listing of the Report Links can be found on pages 116–117 at the back of the book.

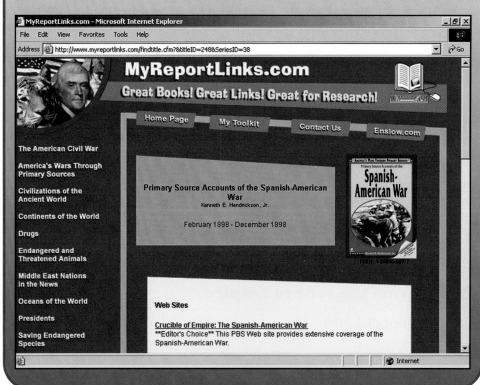

Please see "To Our Readers" on the copyright page for important information about this book, the MyReportLinks.com Web site, and the Report Links that back up this book.

Please enter **PSW1836** if asked for a password.

WHAT ARE PRIMARY SOURCES?

The dead, dying, and wounded are being taken past us to the rear. . . . The bullets . . . are raining into our very faces. The officers . . . decide there is but one thing to do,— Advance! Advance until they find the enemy.

—Lieutenant James A. Moss, Twenty-fifth Infantry, describing the Battle of El Caney, July 1–3, 1898.

The young soldier who wrote these words never dreamed that they would be read by anyone but his family. They were not intended to be read as a history of the Spanish-American War. But his words—and the words of others that have come down to us through scholars or were saved over generations by family members—are unique resources. Historians call such writings primary source documents. As you read this book, you will find other primary source accounts of the war written by the men who fought it. Their letters home reflect their thoughts, their dreams, their fears, and their longing for loved ones. Some of them speak of the excitement of battle, while others mention the everyday boredom of day-to-day life in camp.

But the story of a war is not only the story of the men and women in service. This book also contains diary entries, newspaper accounts, official documents, speeches, and songs of the war years. They reflect the opinions of those who were not in battle but who were still affected by the war. All of these things as well as photographs and art are primary sources—they were created by people who participated in, witnessed, or were affected by the events of the time.

Many of these sources, such as letters and diaries, are a reflection of personal experience. Others, such as newspaper accounts, reflect the mood of the time as well as the opinions of the papers' editors. All of them give us a unique insight into history as it happened. But it is also important to keep in mind that each source reflects its author's biases, beliefs, and background. Each is still someone's interpretation of an event.

Some of the primary sources in this book will be easy to understand; others may not. Their authors came from a different time and were products of different backgrounds and levels of education. So as you read their words, you will see that some of those words may be spelled differently than we would spell them. And some of their stories may be written without the kinds of punctuation we are used to seeing. Each source has been presented as it was originally written, but wherever a word or phrase is unclear or might be misunderstood, an explanation has been added.

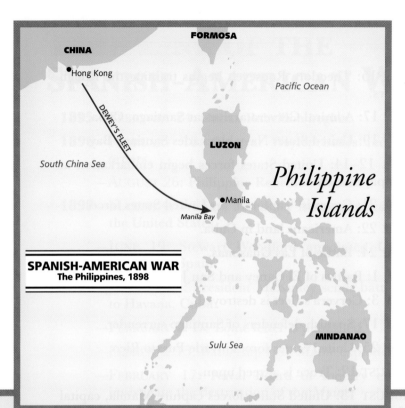

SPANISH-AMERICAN WAR
The Philippines, 1898

FORMOSA

CHINA

● Hong Kong

Pacific Ocean

LUZON

South China Sea

*Philippine
Islands*

● Manila

Manila Bay

MINDANAO

Sulu Sea

DEWEY'S FLEET

SPANISH-AMERICAN WAR
Cuba and Puerto Rico, 1898

● Tampa

FLORIDA

Key West ●

USS *MAINE*
sunk, Feb. 1898

Havana ●

U.S. FLEET

U.S. FLEET

U.S. ARMY

BAHAMA ISLANDS

CUBA

Atlantic Ocean

Caribbean Sea

U.S.
BLOCKADE

Santiago ●

JAMAICA

HAITI

DOMINICAN
REPUBLIC

● San Jua
PUERTO RICO

SPANISH FLEET (CERVERA)

● El Caney

San Juan
Hill

Santiago ●

*Santiago
Harbor*

SPANISH FLEET

U.S.
BLOCKADE

● Las Guasimas

Siboney ● Daiquirí ●

U.S. FLEET

U.S.
Forces

Major battle sites of the Spanish American War.

A HERO IS BORN: THE BATTLE OF MANILA BAY, MAY 1, 1898

Early on the morning of May 1, 1898, Commodore George Dewey, aboard his flagship *Olympia* in Manila Bay, uttered words that would make him famous, "You may fire when you are ready, Captain Gridley."[1] The man who responded was Captain Charles Gridley, commander of the *Olympia*. He repeated the order to the men in the gun turrets, and with that, the Spanish-American War began. Later, it would be called "a splendid little war" by John Hay, the American ambassador to Great Britain. Hay went on to say that . . . "[the war was begun] with the highest motives, carried on with magnificent intelligence and spirit, favored by that fortune which loves the brave."[2]

Although the war, popular with the American people, resulted in the United States acquiring an empire, it was anything but "splendid." It was dirty and bloody and successful only because of the incompetence of the Spanish armed forces, coupled with the unbelievable luck of the Americans. Spain was also fighting thousands of miles away from home to keep colonies that were fighting for their independence. But that is getting ahead of the story.

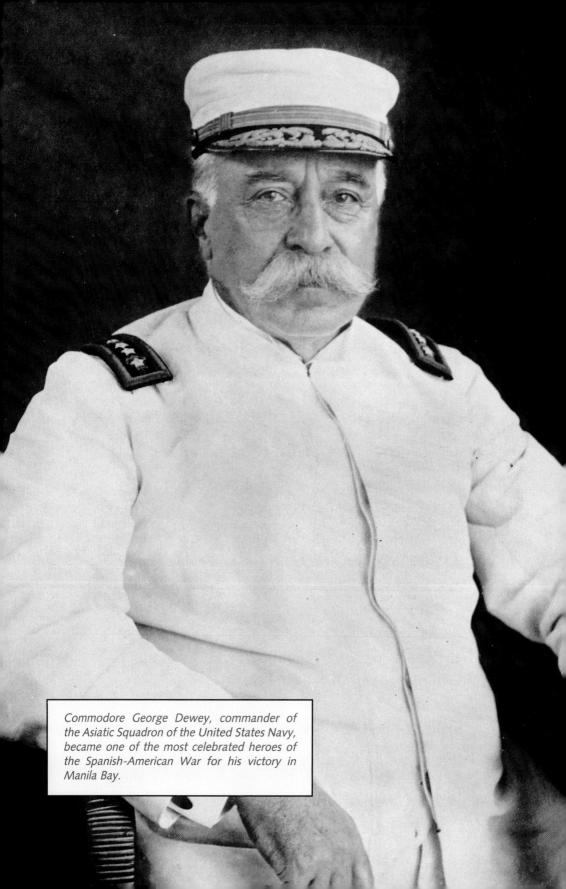

Commodore George Dewey, commander of the Asiatic Squadron of the United States Navy, became one of the most celebrated heroes of the Spanish-American War for his victory in Manila Bay.

Early in 1898, Theodore Roosevelt, an ambitious young politician from New York who favored war with Spain, was serving as assistant secretary of the Navy. One day, while Secretary of the Navy John D. Long was out of the office, Roosevelt issued several orders to naval units around the world. One of these orders went to Commodore George Dewey, commander of the Asiatic Squadron stationed in Hong Kong. Roosevelt told Dewey to get ready to attack the Spanish fleet at Manila, in the Philippines, because he was sure there would soon be war. When Long found out about Roosevelt's actions he was upset, but he did not reverse the orders. He confided his feelings in his diary.

> He [Roosevelt] has gone at things like a bull in a china shop, and with the best purposes in the world has really taken . . . the one course which was most discourteous to me. . . . It shows how the best fellow in the world—and with splendid capacities—is worse than no use if he lacks a cool head and careful discretion.[3]

▶ "War Has Commenced"

As a result of Roosevelt's orders, Dewey was ready to attack the Spaniards when orders to do so arrived on April 25, 1898, from Secretary Long: "War has commenced between the United States and Spain. Proceed at once, . . . particularly against Spanish

Commodore George Dewey Was Born - Microsoft Internet Explorer

File Edit View Favorites Tools Help

Address http://www.americaslibrary.gov/jb/reform/jb_reform_dewey_2_e.html

Captain Gridley aboard the *U.S.S. Olympia*

Captain Charles Gridley aboard the *Olympia* received some of the most famous orders in American naval history when he was asked to fire when ready upon the Spanish fleet in Manila Bay. This image and others can be found on the **Commodore George Dewey** Web page of the Library of Congress.

fleet. You must capture vessels or destroy. Use utmost endeavor."[4]

At about the same time, Basilio Augustin Davila, captain general of the Philippines, issued his own proclamation:

A squadron manned by foreigners, possessing neither instruction nor discipline, is preparing to come to this archipelago with ruffianly intention of robbing us of all that means life, honor, and liberty . . . to treat you as tribes . . . to take possession of your riches. . . . Vain designs! Ridiculous boastings![5]

Davila's words were intended to encourage the men defending Manila and the sailors under the command of Admiral Patricio Montojo. But both men knew they had little chance against the Americans because they were outgunned. As Dewey's fleet, which consisted of nine modern warships, entered Manila Bay on the night of April 30, the commodore called a council of war. Joseph L. Stickney, who was on the *Olympia,* remembered the scene as Dewey issued orders to his captains: "The war council was

▲ The crew of the Olympia *was broken up into groups of twenty to twenty-four men, forming a "mess." The term also applied to the sailors' dining area, next to the galley, or kitchen, on the gun deck. Here, sailors in the* Olympia's *mess eat a meal on tables suspended from ropes.*

of short duration. Commodore Dewey had decided on his plans before it met, and he took little time in giving to each captain his duties for the night and the next day."[6]

The Attack Begins

At 5:40 A.M. on May 1, 1898, when Dewey's ships were about five thousand yards from Montojo's fleet near the shore, the commodore gave his orders, and the *Olympia's* eight-inch guns began the attack. The battle lasted seven hours. When it was done, all the Spanish ships had been sunk or were badly damaged. Firing the guns had been hard work, and Joel E. Evans, a gunner on the *Boston,* remembered the action:

All my men were naked except for shoes and drawers, and I wore only a cotton shirt. . . . Three in the after powder division fainted from the heat. . . . The heat was really fearful. The powder smoke settled down, choking us and half blinding some, and only the love of the work kept us going.[7]

Stickney described the end of the battle:

Soon not one red and yellow ensign remained aloft. . . . The Spanish flagship . . . had long been burning fiercely, and the last Spanish vessel to be abandoned . . . lurched over and sank. Then the Spanish flag . . . was hauled down, and at half past twelve o'clock a white flag [signaling surrender] was hoisted. . . .[8]

BATTLE OF MANILA

▲ The overwhelming American victory in the Battle of Manila Bay was memorialized in song and art not long after the fighting took place. This print is from 1898.

Stickney was certain that Dewey would be the great hero of the war:

It is because Admiral Dewey is a type of the American who compels and deserves the admiration of not only his own countrymen but of the people of every nation who hold dear courage and capacity, delicacy and strength, that his name will go down to posterity as one of the noblest of this century.[9]

The victory did indeed make Dewey an instant national hero. He was promoted to the rank of admiral, and for a short time, a "Dewey for President" movement swept the country. The admiral never became a presidential candidate, but he remained a national hero for the rest of his life.

Chapter 2

A BRIEF HISTORY OF THE WAR

In 1895, the people of both Cuba and the Philippines revolted against Spain, which ruled them. The revolt in the Philippines, an archipelago in the South Pacific, thousands of miles from the American mainland, attracted almost no attention in the United States. Cuba, only ninety miles from Florida's southernmost point, was another matter. By 1895, American businessmen were involved in Cuba, especially in the sugar industry, so instability there concerned the American people and their government. The military operations in Cuba, which involved great savagery by both sides, had also attracted the attention of the American people. American public opinion was overwhelmingly favorable to the Cubans and hostile to the Spanish.

The Spaniards soon discovered that they could not win using conventional methods because the Cubans chose to fight a guerrilla war. So, in February 1896, the Spanish government sent General Valeriano Weyler y Nicolau to Cuba with orders to do whatever was necessary to put down the insurrection. Weyler chose a policy known as reconcentration, which meant that he would force

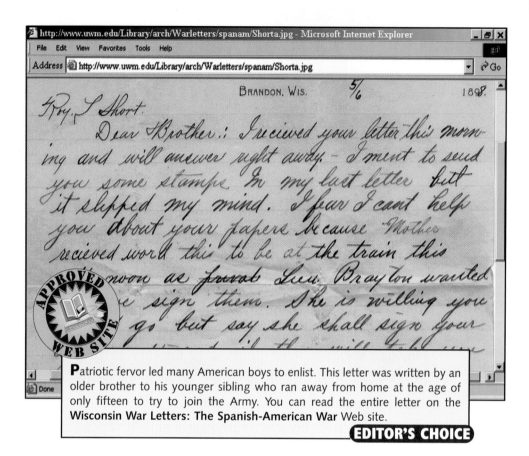

http://www.uwm.edu/Library/arch/Warletters/spanam/Shorta.jpg - Microsoft Internet Explorer

File   Edit   View   Favorites   Tools   Help

Address http://www.uwm.edu/Library/arch/Warletters/spanam/Shorta.jpg

Patriotic fervor led many American boys to enlist. This letter was written by an older brother to his younger sibling who ran away from home at the age of only fifteen to try to join the Army. You can read the entire letter on the **Wisconsin War Letters: The Spanish-American War** Web site.

EDITOR'S CHOICE

entire populations of certain areas to leave their homes and move to concentration camps. There, they could be supervised by the Spanish armed forces. This policy was a failure. The guerrilla fighters continued their attacks, and thousands of innocent people died in the camps. Americans became even more outraged by what was going on in Cuba.

De Lôme Letter

William McKinley, elected president of the United States in 1896, did not want the United States to become involved in the war directly. Instead, he sent

Stewart Woodford, a New York lawyer, to Madrid as his personal representative. Woodford hoped to encourage a negotiated peace, but those hopes were dashed by two events in February 1898. The first event was the so-called De Lôme letter. Enrique Dupuy de Lôme was the Spanish minister to the United States. He knew that many American politicians favored an aggressive policy toward Spain, and he feared that McKinley would give in to the pressure. He voiced his fears in a letter to his friend José Canalejas, who was in Washington, D.C., in December 1897. The letter was stolen and published in William Randolph Hearst's newspaper, the New York *Journal,* on February 9, 1898. In the letter, Dupuy de Lôme wrote the following:

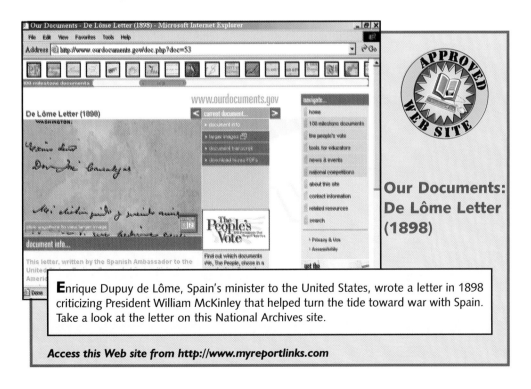

Our Documents: De Lôme Letter (1898)

Enrique Dupuy de Lôme, Spain's minister to the United States, wrote a letter in 1898 criticizing President William McKinley that helped turn the tide toward war with Spain. Take a look at the letter on this National Archives site.

Access this Web site from http://www.myreportlinks.com

Besides the natural and inevitable coarseness with which he [McKinley] repeats all that the press and public opinion of Spain has said of Weyler, it shows once more that McKinley is—weak and catering to the rabble, and, besides, a low politician, who desires to leave a door open to me and to stand well with the jingoes [extreme nationalists who wanted war] of his party.[1]

The publishing of the De Lôme letter was a serious blow to the possibility of a peaceful settlement. John D. Long, McKinley's secretary of the Navy, confided this in his diary on February 10, 1899:

Was obliged to withdraw acceptance of a[n] invitation . . . to dine this evening with the Spanish Minister. It appears that . . . he wrote a private letter in which he made offensive references to the President. This letter has been obtained in some way and published. It, of course, makes the relations of the Spanish Minister with the Administration such that he can no longer remain, and he is obliged to retire from his post. . . . So it is that little things are obstacles that throw great movements off the track and sometimes lead to disaster.[2]

▶ "Remember the *Maine*!"

The second event, which took place just a few days later, was the sinking of the USS *Maine,* an American battleship. Late in January, President McKinley had decided to send an American warship to Havana, Cuba, as a "friendly gesture" as part of an exchange program. Under the command of Captain Charles D. Sigsbee, the *Maine* steamed into the harbor at Havana on January 25, 1898. There the ship sat for three weeks until the night of February 15, when it suddenly blew up, and 266 members of its crew were killed. The blast was almost certainly the result of some internal mechanical malfunction due to poor design, but the American media blamed Spain, calling the disaster an act of sabotage. "Remember the *Maine*!" became a rallying cry for Americans.

Although the American people were generally outraged, there was actually some difference of opinion, as Secretary Long reflected in his diary. On February 16, he wrote:

> There is an intense difference of opinion as to the cause of the blowing up of the *Maine*. In this, as in everything else, the opinion of the individual is determined by his original bias. If he is a conservative, he is sure it was an accident; if he is a jingo, he is equally sure that it was by design. The former is sure that no design could have been carried out without discovery; the latter is equally sure that no accident could have happened in view of the precautions which are taken. My own judgement is . . . that it was the result of an accident. . . . The best way, however, seems to be to suspend judgement until more information shall be had.[3]

▶ Senator Proctor's Speech

In March, Senator Redfield Proctor, a Republican from Vermont, rose to address his colleagues. He had

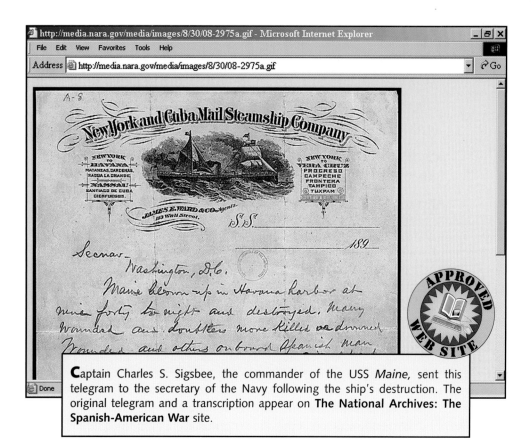

Captain Charles S. Sigsbee, the commander of the USS *Maine*, sent this telegram to the secretary of the Navy following the ship's destruction. The original telegram and a transcription appear on **The National Archives: The Spanish-American War** site.

just returned from a tour of Cuba, and he described what he had seen. Because he was highly respected by conservatives and the business community, his views were taken seriously. They also worked to intensify the demand for war, even though he claimed that had not been his intention. As Proctor said,

I went to Cuba with a strong conviction that the situation had been overdrawn. I could not believe that out of a population of 1,600,000, two hundred thousand had died within these Spanish forts. . . . What I saw I cannot tell so that others can see it. It must be seen with one's own eyes to be realized. . . .

To me the strongest appeal is not the barbarity practiced by Weyler, nor the loss of the *Maine* . . . but the spectacle of a million and a half people, the entire native population of Cuba struggling for freedom and deliverance from the worst misgovernment of which I ever had knowledge.[4]

Intervention

One month later, President McKinley could no longer resist the demands of the public and the leaders of his own party. He asked Congress for the authority to intervene, and his message concluded with these stirring words:

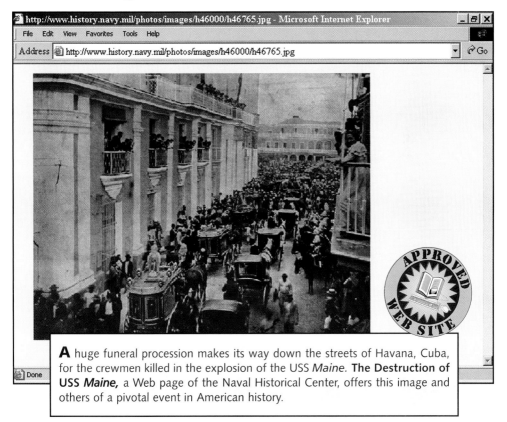

A huge funeral procession makes its way down the streets of Havana, Cuba, for the crewmen killed in the explosion of the USS *Maine*. **The Destruction of USS *Maine*,** a Web page of the Naval Historical Center, offers this image and others of a pivotal event in American history.

In the name of humanity, in the name of civilization, in behalf of endangered American interests which give us the right and the duty to speak and act, the war in Cuba must stop. . . . I ask the Congress to authorize and empower the President to take measures to secure a full and final termination of hostilities between the government of Spain and the people of Cuba, and to secure in the island the establishment of a stable government . . . and to use the military and naval forces of the United States as may be necessary for these purposes. . . .[5]

Teller Amendment

Congress quickly passed a joint resolution that gave McKinley the power to intervene. The resolution included an amendment offered by Senator Henry M. Teller of Colorado, which stated that the United States had no intention of annexing Cuba once the Spanish had been defeated. The Teller Amendment reads as follows:

Whereas the abhorrent [horrible] conditions which have existed for more than three years in the Island of Cuba, so near our own borders, have shocked the moral sense of the people of the United States, have been a disgrace to Christian civilization, culminating, as they have, in the destruction of a United States battle ship, with two hundred and sixty-six of its officers and crew, while on a friendly visit in the harbor of Havana, and cannot longer be endured, as has been set forth by the President of the United States in his message to Congress of April eleventh, eighteen

there, so that is where most of the organizational nightmares occurred. This city of 26,000 people located on the Gulf of Mexico was selected as the point of departure because it had a port and was the closest available site to Cuba. But it had many disadvantages. Only two railroads reached the city from the north, and only one connected the city to Port Tampa nine miles to the south. All supplies had to be transported to Tampa by rail and then unloaded and reloaded to be taken to the port facilities. There they had to be unloaded and reloaded again on the transports that would take them to Cuba. Tons of supplies

Our Boys in Camp--Writing a Letter for Home. - Microsoft Internet Explorer

File   Edit   View   Favorites   Tools   Help

Address http://fcit.usf.edu/florida/photos/military/saw/saw2/saw216.htm

Tampa, Florida, was the training ground for American soldiers who went on to fight in Cuba. Here, soldiers in camp write letters home to loved ones before boarding ships. This image and others are found on the **Spanish-American War Gallery** Web site of the University of South Florida.

eventually arrived, but they often did not find their way to the soldiers.

On to Cuba

General William R. Shafter commanded the American forces that were to invade Cuba. In spite of all the confusion, he did his best to prepare them for action. They were not ready, but they were eager when the orders came to go in early June. The trouble was that there were 20,000 men in Tampa and room for only 16,000 on the available transport ships. So there was a mad scramble to get from Tampa to Port Tampa to secure space for the voyage. Theodore Roosevelt and the Rough Riders were as determined as any to go. Roosevelt described in his memoirs how they seized transportation:

At last, however, after an hour's industrious and rapid search through this ant-heap of humanity, Wood and I, who had separated, found Colonel Humphrey at nearly the same time and were allotted a transport—the *Yucatan*. She was out in midstream, so Wood seized a stray launch and boarded her. At the same time I happened to find out that she had been allotted to two other regiments, the Second Regular Infantry and the Seventy-First New York Volunteers. . . . Accordingly, I ran at full speed to our train; and leaving a strong guard with the baggage I double-quicked the rest of the regiment up to the boat just in time to board her as she came into the quay and then to hold her against the Second Regulars and the Seventy-First, who had arrived a little too late. . . .[9]

Once they were aboard, rumors that a Spanish naval squadron had been sighted in the Gulf of Mexico caused a delay. A full week passed before they actually departed, and conditions on the over-crowded ships were horrible. Roosevelt was enraged:

> The steamer on which we are contains nearly one thousand men, there being room for about five hundred comfortably . . . several companies are down in the lower hold, which is unpleasantly suggestive of the Black Hole of Calcutta. . . . Now, if this were necessary no one would complain for a moment. . . . But it is absolutely unnecessary; the five day's great heat and crowded confinement are telling visibly upon the spirits and health of the troops.[10]

The "Black Hole of Calcutta" that Roosevelt referred to was a dungeon in India where more than one hundred British prisoners of war were alleged to have suffocated after being captured by Indian troops in the eighteenth century.

Las Guasimas

When it was finally determined that there was no Spanish squadron in the area, the Americans set off for Cuba. A few days later, they went ashore at Daiquirí and Siboney, two small towns a few miles east of Santiago. Miraculously, there was no opposition. On June 24, American troops fought a bloody skirmish with Spanish forces at the village of

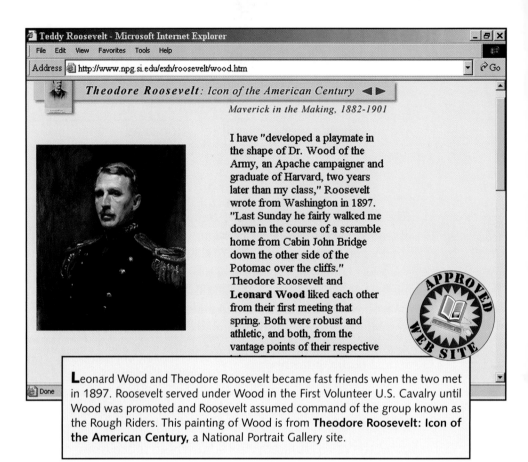

Teddy Roosevelt - Microsoft Internet Explorer

File   Edit   View   Favorites   Tools   Help

Address http://www.npg.si.edu/exh/roosevelt/wood.htm   Go

Theodore Roosevelt: Icon of the American Century ◄ ►

Maverick in the Making, 1882-1901

I have "developed a playmate in the shape of Dr. Wood of the Army, an Apache campaigner and graduate of Harvard, two years later than my class," Roosevelt wrote from Washington in 1897. "Last Sunday he fairly walked me down in the course of a scramble home from Cabin John Bridge down the other side of the Potomac over the cliffs." Theodore Roosevelt and **Leonard Wood** liked each other from their first meeting that spring. Both were robust and athletic, and both, from the vantage points of their respective

Done

Leonard Wood and Theodore Roosevelt became fast friends when the two met in 1897. Roosevelt served under Wood in the First Volunteer U.S. Cavalry until Wood was promoted and Roosevelt assumed command of the group known as the Rough Riders. This painting of Wood is from **Theodore Roosevelt: Icon of the American Century,** a National Portrait Gallery site.

Las Guasimas. Although the action was unnecessary to the overall strategy of the expedition, it did boost the Americans' morale. The Americans were now more convinced than ever that they could defeat the Spaniards. The basic plan was to capture the city of Santiago, which was defended by the bulk of the Spanish Army. Between the Americans and the city lay several Spanish strong points, however, and the most dangerous of these were the village of El Caney, Kettle Hill, and San Juan Heights. These had to be captured first.

El Caney, the Hills, and Puerto Rico

The assault on El Caney and the hills took place on July 1, one of the most important days of the war as well as one of the bloodiest days. General Shafter, who at 300 pounds had difficulty getting up on his horse, assigned the attack to a division under the command of General Henry W. Lawton. Securing El Caney was supposed to take about two hours, but the Spaniards put up a much stiffer resistance than expected, and the village did not fall until well after noon. The attack on the hills began about 1:00 P.M. Forces under Generals Hamilton S. Hawkins and Jacob F. Kent stormed up San Juan Hill, while dismounted cavalry, including Teddy Roosevelt and the Rough Riders, took

This print commemorates the U.S. Marines raising an American flag on June 11, 1898, for the first time on Cuban soil.

Kettle Hill. The fighting here was savage, with heavy casualties on both sides, but by the end of the day, the Americans controlled both positions. Then there was a standoff for the next two weeks until the Spaniards were persuaded to surrender. After that, an expedition under General Nelson A. Miles was dispatched to Puerto Rico. There was little actual combat in Puerto Rico, and the Americans were in control even before the armistice was signed on August 12.

▶ Santiago Bay

Earlier, President McKinley had ordered a blockade of Cuba to prevent supplies and reinforcements from reaching the Spanish forces there. The North Atlantic Squadron, under the command of Admiral William T. Sampson, was sent to enforce the blockade while a second battle group known as the Flying Squadron, under the command of Admiral Winfield Scott Schley, was assigned to protect the east coast.

At the same time, a Spanish fleet under the command of Admiral Pascual Cervera y Topete left Spain bound for the Caribbean. Cervera's force consisted of seven obsolete ships. He knew that if he ever had to engage the Americans, his fleet would be destroyed. He was determined to do his duty for his country, but he was also reluctant to undertake the mission that he considered a lost cause.

Do we not owe to our country not only our life, if necessary, but the exposition of our beliefs? I am very uneasy about this. I ask myself if it is right . . . to . . . make myself an accomplice in adventures which will surely cause the total ruin of Spain. And for what purpose? To defend an island which was ours, but belongs to us no more, because even if we did not lose it by right in the war we have lost it in fact, and with it all our wealth and an enormous number of young men . . . in the defense of what is now no more than a romantic idea.[11]

As soon as he could, Cervera took his ships into Santiago Bay, where he would be safe temporarily. When the Americans learned of this, they sent both squadrons to blockade the mouth of the bay and trap Cervera. On the morning of Sunday, July 3,

http://www.loc.gov/rr/hispanic/1898/img/cerveraold.jpg - Microsoft Internet Explorer

Admiral Pascual Cervera commanded the small, outdated fleet of Spanish ships defending Cuba during the war. **The World of 1898: The Spanish-American War,** a Library of Congress Web site, offers this image of Cervera as well as many other photographs from the era.

EDITOR'S CHOICE

after the Americans had taken the heights above Santiago, Admiral Cervera was ordered to sail out and fight. Beginning at 9:30 that morning, his ships came out one at a time and immediately turned west in an effort to escape. They were much too slow, and the Americans soon caught up. During the next two hours, all the Spanish ships were destroyed. When Secretary Long heard of this great naval victory, he, with the rest of the country, was overjoyed:

> I can give you very little idea of the intense excitement here, and the feeling of triumph which is in the air. I do hope that Spain will see the idleness of further contest, and that we are on the eve of peace.[12]

The Philippines

The last act of the war took place in the Philippines, where Commodore Dewey had won his great victory in May. He had destroyed the Spanish fleet, but ground troops were needed to defeat the Spaniards defending Manila. A large force under the command of General Wesley Merritt set sail in June, with one of the ships stopping to take possession of the island of Guam. Merritt had orders to force the Spaniards to surrender. He was also ordered not to enter into an alliance with Emilio Aguinaldo y Famy, the Filipino Nationalist leader who had been fighting for independence from Spain before the Spanish-American War started. The United States had no intention of

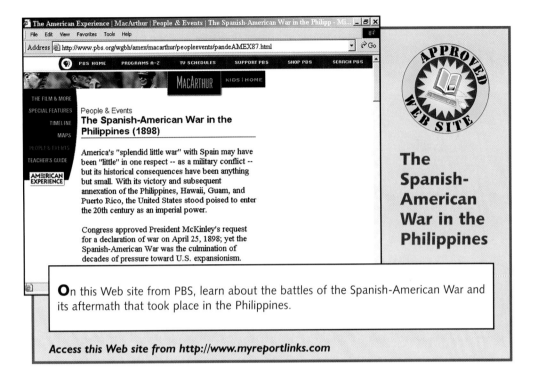

The American Experience | MacArthur | People & Events | The Spanish-American War in the Philipp - Mi...

File   Edit   View   Favorites   Tools   Help

Address http://www.pbs.org/wgbh/amex/macarthur/peopleevents/pandeAMEX87.html   Go

PBS HOME   PROGRAMS A-Z   TV SCHEDULES   SUPPORT PBS   SHOP PBS   SEARCH PBS

MacArthur   KIDS | HOME

THE FILM & MORE

SPECIAL FEATURES   People & Events

TIMELINE   **The Spanish-American War in the Philippines (1898)**

MAPS

PEOPLE & EVENTS

TEACHER'S GUIDE   America's "splendid little war" with Spain may have been "little" in one respect -- as a military conflict -- but its historical consequences have been anything but small. With its victory and subsequent annexation of the Philippines, Hawaii, Guam, and Puerto Rico, the United States stood poised to enter the 20th century as an imperial power.

AMERICAN EXPERIENCE

Congress approved President McKinley's request for a declaration of war on April 25, 1898; yet the Spanish-American War was the culmination of decades of pressure toward U.S. expansionism.

The Spanish-American War in the Philippines

On this Web site from PBS, learn about the battles of the Spanish-American War and its aftermath that took place in the Philippines.

Access this Web site from http://www.myreportlinks.com

recognizing Philippine independence, Secretary of State William R. Day explained:

> The United States in entering upon the occupation of the islands as a result of its military operations in that quarter, will do so in the exercise of the rights which the state of war confers, and will expect from the inhabitants . . . that obedience which will be lawfully due from them.[13]

Don Fermín Jáudenes y Alvarez, the Spanish commander, knew he could not defeat the Americans and wanted to surrender to them, hoping they would protect him and his men from the Filipinos. But he had to put up some hint of a struggle in order to defend Spanish honor. So, Jáudenes proposed a sham battle in which he would only appear to fight if the Americans would agree to keep the Filipinos out of the city. Merritt agreed, and the charade took place on the morning of August 13. Unfortunately, there was some firing by nervous participants, and both sides suffered a few casualties, but by early afternoon the Americans entered the city.

▶ Spain Surrenders the Philippines

Aguinaldo and his men were left out, and the Filipino leader was angry. Aguinaldo had been named the president in 1897 of a revolutionary government in the Philippines and helped draft a constitution for the Filipino people. He had agreed to go into exile in return for the Spanish government's granting of certain rights to Filipinos. Following the Americans' victory in Manila Bay in 1898, Aguinaldo had returned to his country but soon grew upset with what he correctly saw would be an extended American military presence there.

The formal terms of surrender were signed by Merritt and Jáudenes on August 14. Neither man was aware that the "battle" had actually taken place after the signing of a peace protocol in Washington on August 12. This situation raised questions of international law because if the victory occurred after the signing of the protocol, then technically the islands had not been conquered. This problem was resolved later at a peace conference in Paris.

VOICES OF WAR: THE COMBATANTS SPEAK

When American transport ships reached Cuba, the water was too shallow for them to come in close, so the soldiers, with all their equipment, had to be rowed to shore in small boats. Their horses had to swim. Captain John Bigelow, Jr., of the Tenth Cavalry, an African-American unit, remembered the landing in his bitter memoir:

> The landing of men went on the rest of the day. The mules for the wagons and pack-trains were mostly thrown overboard and left to swim ashore, and few I understand, were lost. This afternoon (June 22) our regiment went from the *Leona* onto a large tug, which took us to the . . . dock at which we landed. Many of the men had to jump from the vessel to the dock, and afterwards from plank to plank. Two . . . had already been drowned here, and it is a wonder that no more were lost.[1]

The first action took place near the village of Las Guasimas on June 24, when Major General Joseph Wheeler ordered his men to attack the Spanish defenders. Captain Bigelow remembered the fight:

 The village of Las Guasimas was the site of the first fighting of the war in Cuba. Two cavalry units, the Ninth and Tenth, supported the Rough Riders there.

The ground was admirably adapted to the purpose for what the enemy had chosen it. . . . The country was generally covered with dense wood and under-growth. Immediately adjoining the creek were a few acres of completely level, open ground. . . .

Our men deployed under a galling fire, and rapidly advanced, firing at will. The enemy was formed in two lines. . . . The two lines numbered about twenty-four hundred men. . . . About half an hour after the battle opened, the fire of the Rough Riders was heard on the left. . . . The enemy retreated in time to prevent our taking any prisoners, but leaving a number of their dead where they fell.[2]

The leader of the Cuban insurgents, General Máximo Gómez, was not present at Las Guasimas. When he heard of the skirmish, he did not think it important. He confided to his diary:

Encamped . . . same place June has ended without our learning about any important occurrence. The news that the Americans are attacking heavily along the sea at Santiago de Cuba is being emphasized.[3]

El Caney and San Juan

The most important land battles of the war took place on July 1. These were the attacks on El Caney and Kettle and San Juan hills. The men who participated in those attacks had vivid memories of the day. Lieutenant James A. Moss of the Twenty-fifth Infantry, an African-American regiment, described the Battle of El Caney as he saw it:

The dead, dying, and wounded are being taken past to the rear; the wounded and their attendants are telling the Twenty-fifth: "Give them hell, boys; they've been doing us dirt all morning.". . . The Spaniards are using smokeless powder . . . we cannot locate them. . . . The bullets . . . are raining into our very faces. The officers . . . decide there is but one thing to do,—Advance! Advance until they find the enemy.

Our firing line is now no more than one hundred and fifty yards from the fort. . . . The Spaniards are shaken and demoralized. . . . A young officer is running up and down . . . exclaiming to the men in the

▲ *These African-American soldiers were photographed at Camp Wikoff, on Montauk Point, Long Island, where they and some other American forces returning from Cuba were quarantined. The U.S. Army set up this camp to prevent the spread of malaria, yellow fever, typhoid fever, and other infectious diseases that soldiers had contracted during the war.*

rear: "Come on, Come on, men —we've got 'em on the run. Remember the *Maine!*"[4]

James F. J. Archibald described the end of the fight:

The enemy's last stand was at the little thatched fort . . . at the western entrance of the town . . . where a small band of Spaniards held the road for hours and died like heroes. . . . Their officers appeared to court death. . . .[5]

General Joaquín Vara del Rey, one of the Spanish officers, was killed near the end of the battle. The Americans buried him with military honors. A member of his staff was moved by that action.

> I have never seen anything to equal the courage and dash of those Americans, who, stripped to the waist, offering their naked breasts to our murderous fire, literally threw themselves on our trenches—on the very muzzles of our guns. We had the advantage of position, and mowed them down by the hundreds, but they never retreated or fell back. . . . Their gallantry was heroic.[6]

Captain Arthur Lee, the British military attaché, agreed although he believed the attack had not been well planned.

> This was a heavy price to pay for the possession of an outlying fort, defended by an inferior force, but it only bore out the well-known military axiom [saying] that the attack on a fortified village cannot succeed, without great loss of life, unless the assailants are strong in artillery. . . . That the attack succeeded was entirely due to the magnificent courage and endurance of the infantry officers and men.[7]

The attack on Kettle Hill and San Juan Hill began in the afternoon, several hours after it was supposed to happen. Rough Rider Frank Knox, who went on to a distinguished career in government, remembered how the assault began.

▲ *Frank Knox, a Rough Rider who also served in World War I, went on to a distinguished career in both the public and private sectors. A newspaper correspondent, a newspaper owner, and the Republican vice-presidential nominee in 1936, he was named by President Franklin Delano Roosevelt in 1940 to be the secretary of the Navy.*

The enemy were slowly withdrawing from the brush into the bottoms of the trenches on the hills. As they withdrew, we advanced on our hands and knees, crawling on our stomachs at times, and where the ground permitted, with a rush, until we had driven them all to the hilltops. Now began the serious work of the day. We had to dislodge an enemy our equal or superior in numbers from a strongly fortified and entrenched position on the ranges of hills that surround the city.[8]

General E. J. McClernand, who was an assistant to General Shafter, remembered the assault on the hills in glowing terms:

In the fierce fighting for the Heights words fail to do justice to the magnificent training and courage of the . . . company commanders and their men. . . . It was, after all, the intrepid dash and bravery of the subordinate officers and men that carried our flag to the summit of San Juan Hill and thus sealed the fate of Santiago.[9]

Theodore Roosevelt also lavished praise on his men, the famous Rough Riders:

In less than sixty days the regiment had been raised, organized, armed, equipped, drilled, mounted, dismounted, kept for a fortnight on transports, and put through two victorious aggressive fights in very difficult country, the loss in killed and wounded amounting to a quarter of those engaged. This is a record which it is not easy to match in the history of volunteer organizations. . . . It must be remembered they were already good individual fighters, skilled in the use of horse and rifle, so that there was no need of putting them through the same kind of training in which the ordinary raw recruit must spend his first year or two.[10]

One of the men who participated in the charge was Charles Johnson Post of the Seventy-first New York Volunteers. He remembered the importance of the battle:

This hill and ridge of San Juan was the key to Santiago. The Spaniards could not afford to let us hold it. Yet no counterattack came! It was less than a mile to the first lanes of straggling red-roofed houses of the

▲ *A United States Army artillery battery's cannons fire on the stone fort at El Caney, a small village northeast of Santiago, Cuba.*

city. It was two miles to the water front of the bay where lay Admiral Cervera's Spanish fleet. . . . Had we men enough to hold the Hill? It was an officer's worry, not ours. We had no doubts, then or later.[11]

Santiago Bay

After crossing the Atlantic with his little fleet, Admiral Cervera had taken refuge in Santiago Bay. On Sunday, July 3, 1898, he was ordered to leave the bay and engage the American fleet. Cervera knew there was no hope of victory, and he did not want to take responsibility for a foolish act. But he was determined to do his duty.

I state most emphatically that I shall never be the one to decree the horrible and useless hetacomb [horrible event] which will be the only possible result of the sortie from here by main forces, for I should consider myself responsible before God and history for their lives, sacrificed on the altar of vanity, and not in the true defense of the country.[12]

As the Spanish ships steamed out of the harbor at about 9:30 in the morning, Captain Robley D. Evans of the American battleship *Iowa* recorded his reaction.

I had just finished my breakfast, and was sitting smoking at my cabin table, in conversation with my son, a naval cadet, . . . [when] . . . the general alarm for action rang all over the ship. . . . We both started as fast as we could go for the bridge . . . at this moment the Spanish cruiser *Infanta María Teresa* was in plain view . . . her magnificent battle flag just showing clear . . . as I reached the bridge.[13]

Captain Victor Concas, commander of Cervera's flagship, remembered the same moment as he received permission to fire.

The sound of my bugles was the last echo of those which history tells us were sounded at the capture of Granada. It was the signal that the history of four centuries of grandeur was at an end and that Spain was becoming a nation of the fourth class.[14]

By noon the slaughter was over. Little damage had been done to the American fleet, but all the Spanish ships were destroyed or disabled. Lieutenant Jose Müller y Tejeria, a Spanish naval officer, recalled his emotions: "If I were to live a thousand years and a thousand centuries never should I forget that 3rd day of July, 1898, nor do I believe that Spain will ever forget it."[15]

Lieutenant Joaquín Bustamante, executive officer of the Spanish destroyer *Furor*, recorded the sinking of his ship:

When we got to the bay's mouth, we saw our squadron [Cervera's four cruisers had exited the bay previous to the *Furor* and *Pluton*], and decided, that if we went to west, we could gain the protection of our squadron.

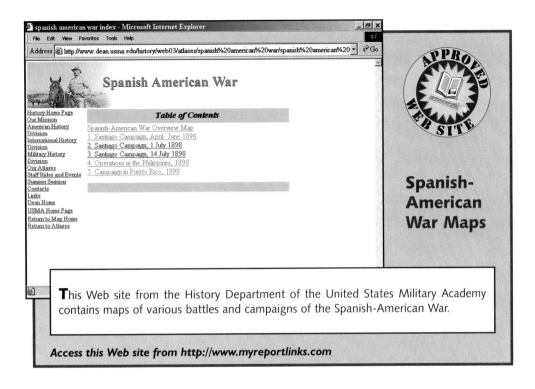

Spanish-American War Maps

This Web site from the History Department of the United States Military Academy contains maps of various battles and campaigns of the Spanish-American War.

Access this Web site from http://www.myreportlinks.com

But there was some distance between us and [the] squadron. One shell hit on our hatch, where our boiler's ventilators were located, so our steam pressure reduced considerably, and our speed slowed. At this time we had suffered a great quantity of hits. One shell cut up the boatswain in half and the part of his body fell into the steering control line. As a result of this, the ship lost partial rudder control. We needed to clear the body from the steering control line. . . .

We had torpedoes cleared for action. . . . but we were unable to fire because, the distance was too great during the battle. As a result of these circumstances the commander of both destroyers, Capitan de Navio Villamil ordered us to abandon ship. Myself and part of the crew leaped overboard about three miles off the coast.

In the water I saw one of my comrades . . . was killed by a bullet to the head. At this time our destroyer, after a series of explosions, sank. When we got to the coast, we went on foot east toward Santiago. Shortly afterwards, we met the men of Lieutenant Caballero [senior officer of the *Terror*] and together proceeded to Santiago.[16]

Admiral William Thomas Sampson sent the following message to the White House: "The fleet under my command offers the nation as a Fourth of July present the whole of Cervera's fleet."[17]

Surrender of Santiago

Two weeks after the great naval battle, General José Toral, commander of the Spanish forces at Santiago, surrendered. Major General Joseph Wheeler described the surrender ceremony:

General Shafter, together with the generals and their staffs, rode to a large field in front of Santiago. . . . There they met General Toral, who was also accompanied by a company of one hundred men. . . . General Shafter . . . presented him with the sword and spurs of the Spanish General Vara del Rey, who was killed at El Caney. The Spanish troops then presented arms, and the Spanish flag, which for three hundred and eighty-two years had floated over the city, was pulled down and furled forever.[18]

About a month later, before they were evacuated, the Spanish soldiers who had defended Santiago sent a farewell message to the Americans. Even though they did not think that they had been on the losing side, they congratulated the Americans

▲ *Wounded Spanish prisoners of war at a makeshift hospital on San Juan Hill.*

and sent them good wishes. This document ranks as one of the most unusual in the history of modern warfare.

We would not be fulfilling our duty as well-born men in whose breasts there live gratitude and courtesy should we embark for our beloved Spain without sending to you our most cordial and sincere good wishes and farewell. We fought you with ardor, with all our strength, endeavoring to gain the victory, but without the slightest rancor or hate towards the American nation. We have been vanquished by you (so our generals and chiefs judged in signing the capitulation), but our surrender and the bloody battle preceding it have left in our souls no place for resentment against the men who fought us nobly and valiantly. You fought and acted in compliance with the same call of duty as we, for we all represent the power of our respective States. You fought us as men face to face and with great courage, as before stated, a quality which we had not met with during the three years we have carried on this war against a people without religion, without morals, without conscience and of doubtful origin, who could not confront the enemy, but, hidden, shot their noble victims from ambush and then immediately fled. This was the kind of warfare we had to sustain in this unfortunate land.

You have complied exactly with all the laws and usages of war as recognized by the armies of the most civilized nations of the world; have given honorable burial to the dead of the vanquished; have cured their wounded with great humanity; have respected and cared for your prisoners and their comfort; and, lastly, to us, whose condition was terrible, you have, given freely of food, of your stock of medicines, and you have honored us with distinction and courtesy, for

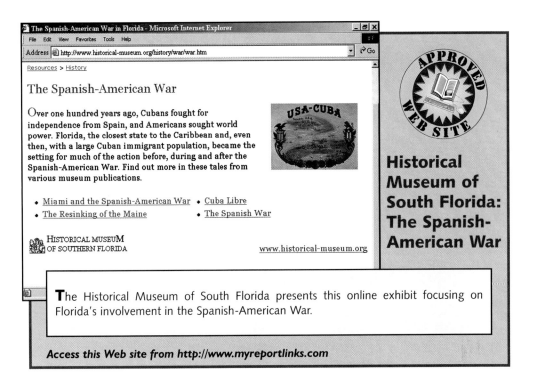

The Spanish-American War in Florida - Microsoft Internet Explorer

File   Edit   View   Favorites   Tools   Help

Address http://www.historical-museum.org/history/war/war.htm   Go

Resources > History

The Spanish-American War

Over one hundred years ago, Cubans fought for
independence from Spain, and Americans sought world
power. Florida, the closest state to the Caribbean and, even
then, with a large Cuban immigrant population, became the
setting for much of the action before, during and after the
Spanish-American War. Find out more in these tales from
various museum publications.

- Miami and the Spanish-American War   • Cuba Libre
- The Resinking of the Maine   • The Spanish War

HISTORICAL MUSEUM
OF SOUTHERN FLORIDA   www.historical-museum.org

Historical Museum of South Florida: The Spanish-American War

The Historical Museum of South Florida presents this online exhibit focusing on Florida's involvement in the Spanish-American War.

Access this Web site from http://www.myreportlinks.com

after the fighting the two armies mingled with the utmost harmony.

With the high sentiment of appreciation from us all, there remains but to express our farewell, and with the greatest sincerity we wish you all happiness and health in this land, which will no longer belong to our, dear Spain but will be yours, who have conquered it by force and watered it with your blood as your conscience called for, under the demand of civilization and humanity.

From 11,000 Spanish soldiers
Pedro Lopez de Castillo, Soldier of Infantry
Santiago de Cuba, August 21, 1898.[19]

The Cubans, who were supposed to be allies of the Americans, were not invited to participate in the surrender ceremony or enter the city of Santiago. Maximo Gómez, their leader, was outraged, as he confided to his diary:

> . . . it was such an uncivil act which the American officers committed. . . . Their ignorance is so dense that it didn't permit them to perceive that in light of our own history the considerations and respect we deserve. . . . To fail to respect one of our Generals . . . only occurs to a drunk and brutal American.[20]

Puerto Rico

Another army under General Nelson A. Miles had sailed to Puerto Rico in July. Miles was ordered to that Caribbean island, once ruled by Spain, to secure it for the United States. One of Miles's men, George G. King, kept a diary of his adventures. King's first emotion was boredom:

> Life aboard ship was becoming very irksome. In civilian life the *Yale* was [a passenger liner]. She was assigned to transport duty solely in an emergency, and with no notion that we would remain on board more than three or four days. There were about 1500 of us. The main deck and the steerage were crowded.[21]

When they landed at Guánica on the southwestern coast of the island, they met no opposing force, but they did meet with danger.

> There were no docks at Guánica. . . . We took advantage of the excellent bathing until someone yelled "shark." In the shallow water it was doubtful whether swimming or floundering was more expeditious, but by one method or the other or a combination of both, several hundred men emerged from the water with amazing speed.[22]

King saw no action although he was in Puerto Rico until October. After arriving home in Boston, he was offered a staff position in the Philippines, but he declined: "I concluded rather against my desire that a military life in peace time would be aimless and

Illinois Citizen-Soldier: A Look Through Time, a Web site of the Illinois State Military Museum, provides information on the men from Illinois who served in the Spanish-American War.

uninteresting."[23] That decision may have saved his life, because service in the Philippines after the Spanish surrender was anything but peaceful.

What little fighting occurred in Puerto Rico took place between August 5 and August 12. The most serious engagement was fought near the village of Coamo on August 7. Richard Harding Davis, a journalist who accompanied the Americans to Puerto Rico, described the action:

> The white helmet of the general (General James H. Wilson) halted next to an open field of high yellow grass, where four brown guns pointed at a block-house on the hill above Coamo. As we drew up one of the guns roared and flashed, and a cloud of white smoke rushed forward. . . . A few Mauser rifles answered, . . . but the bullets flew high and did no harm. . . .
>
> The Spanish commandante seemed to wish to die. He galloped out of the road and into the meadow, where he was conspicuous. . . . After he was killed the men in the trench along the road raised a white handkerchief on a stick and ceased firing. . . .[24]

The Americans suffered so few casualties in Puerto Rico that some American journalists, including Finley Peter Dunne, a newspaperman from Chicago, made fun of the invasion. Dunne had created a fictional character named Martin J. Dooley, an Irish bartender. Mr. Dooley talked about important events with his friend, Mr. Hennessy, usually in sarcastic terms. He referred to the conquest of Puerto Rico as "General Miles's Moonlight Excursion."

"Dear, oh, dear;" said Mr. Dooley, "I'd give five dollars— an' I'd kill a man f'r three—if I was out iv this Sixth Wa-ard tonight, an' down with Gin'ral Miles' gran' picnic an' moonlight excursion in Porther Ricky [Puerto Rico]. 'Tis no comfort in bein' a cow'rd whin ye think iv thim br-rave la-ads facin' death be suffication in bokays an' dyin' iv waltzin' with th' pretty girls iv Porther Ricky. . . .

BOMBARDMENT OF SAN JUAN.
PORTO RICO.

▲ On May 12, 1898, the harbor of San Juan, Puerto Rico, was bombarded by American ships commanded by William T. Sampson.

"I'd hate to tell ye iv th' thriles iv th' expedition, Hinnissy. Whin th' picnic got as far as Punch, on th' southern coast iv Porther Ricky, Gin'ral Miles gazes out, an' says he, 'This looks like a good place to hang th' hammicks, an' have lunch,' says he. 'Forward, brave men,' says he, 'where ye see me di'mon's sparkles' says he. 'Forward, an' plant th' crokay ar-rches iv our beloved counthry,' he says. An' in they wint, like inthrepid warryors that they ar-re. . . .

"Th' flex' day th' army moved on Punch; an' Gin'ral Miles marched into th' ill-fated city, preceded be flower-girls sthrewin' r-roses an' geranyums befure him. In th' afthernoon they was a lawn tinnis party, an' at night the gin'ral attinded a banket at th Gran' Palace Hotel. At midnight he was serenaded be th' Raymimber th' *Maine* Banjo an' Mandolin Club. Th' entire popylace attinded, with pork chops in their buttonholes to show their pathreetism [patriotism]."[25]

Dunne's characterization of General Miles tended to make the public view the general as less than a hero. Richard Harding Davis, a war correspondent whose coverage was colorful if not always accurate, believed this conclusion was unfair.

The reason the Spanish bull gored our men in Cuba and failed to touch them in Porto [sic] Rico was entirely due to the fact that Miles was an expert matador; so it was hardly fair to the commanding General and the gentle-men under him to send the Porto [sic] Rican campaign down into history as a picnic.[26]

The Philippines

After Admiral Dewey defeated the Spanish fleet in Manila Bay, Emilio Aguinaldo, the Filipino leader, proclaimed independence: "Now that the great and powerful North American nation have come to offer disinterested protection for the effort to secure the liberation of this country, I return to assume command of all the forces for the attainment of our lofty aspirations."[27] But the American government had other ideas.

▲ When the United States claimed victory over Spain in the Philippines, Emilio Aguinaldo (front row, third from right) hoped his dream of Filipino independence would come true. When he realized that the United States had no intention of liberating the islands, he led a force against American troops.

By the end of June 1898, there were nearly eleven thousand American troops in the Philippines under the command of Major General Wesley Merritt. He had been ordered to take Manila without involving the Filipinos. Fermín Jáudenes, the Spanish commander, wanted to surrender and be protected from the Filipinos, but was honor bound to offer some resistance. So he and Merritt agreed to stage a sham battle, but, due to poor communications, the battle was not without some loss of life. Trooper Frank David Millet reported:

> Without waiting . . . [General Greene], followed by a half dozen of us who were mounted, galloped up the street . . . In a few minutes we reached a heavy barricade. . . . Here . . . an officer and a private soldier appeared. . . . General Greene asked him if the town had surrendered, and he replied that he did not know, as he had simply been ordered to put up the white flag.[28]

Soon, the firing stopped and the real surrender took place. Neither side knew that an armistice agreement had been reached twenty-four hours earlier between Spain and the United States.

▶ Coming Home

Disease had claimed the lives of more American soldiers fighting in Cuba than their Spanish counterparts did. General Shafter knew he had to get his men off the island as soon as possible, and the evacuation soon began. But it was not pleasant. The men were loaded onto transport ships bound for New York. Charles Johnson Post remembered the trip:

> There were not ten men in the company fit for duty or even fit to be out of a hospital—a hospital at home. . . . Next morning we went aboard the . . . transport *Grand Duchesse*. . . . There were no mattresses, pillows, or sheets. The bunks were bare boards. . . .
>
> Distilled water was issued twice a day. . . . There was no water in which to wash our tin cups or our shallow mess tins, and both were rancid with old grease. . . .

▲ *A surgeon with the United States Army treats wounded soldiers in the field during the war.*

There was . . . a mess for those strong enough to get to it, but it was hardly worth while . . . for they served canned corned beef, hardtack hash, and coffee. . . .

The whole ship was septic with dysentery. . . . And our deck . . . was crowded with such men. . . . There was but one latrine . . . It was wholly inadequate for the thousand men now on board the *Grand Duchesse*. . . .

After several days of torment, they reached Long Island.

Then, on one slow, sweet cool of dawn, we saw against the horizon the low, purple silhouette of the hill of

At the **National Museum of Health & Medicine: Spanish-American War** site, an online exhibit examines the Army's health-care system at the time of the Spanish-American War. Archival images are featured, such as this one of nurses who served on the United States hospital ship *Relief*.

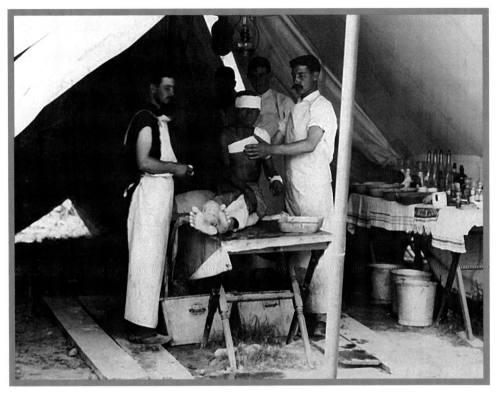

▲ *Filipinos were cared for in the "Filipino Ward" of this Army Division Hospital in 1899.*

Montauk Point, Long Island. . . . We were home. The quarantine hospital was on a little plateau that rested on top of a high hill overlooking Montauk Bay. . . .

We saw the tents and knew we would be assigned to them. . . . It is difficult to realize the utter emptiness of time in those days. We measured time in food; in the time between chills; and when the fever left us . . . we measured it in dysentery, and in latrines.

Finally, he got a pass to go to New York City. There he was able to get cleaned up, get adequate food, and get medical attention. "I was lucky," he wrote. "I had survived."[29]

▶ Medical Advances

As terrible as the conditions were during the Spanish-American War, even more Americans would have succumbed to disease and battle injuries if not for certain advances in medicine. Doctors and nurses working in temporary military hospitals had become better trained in antiseptic practices, meaning infections were not introduced or spread by them. The 1895 discovery of X-rays meant that bullets could be found much more easily than before, without doctors probing the wounds of soldiers. Sterile operating rooms also meant fewer amputations. The mortality rate of wounded soldiers in the Spanish-American War was half as great as it had been in the Civil War, thanks to improved techniques and conditions.[30]

In 1900, an Army commission in Cuba was determined to make conditions there safer for the Americans who had stayed on as an occupying force. Army captain Dr. Walter Reed and his team were able to identify a mosquito as the agent transmitting the yellow fever virus to humans. That disease, along with typhoid fever and dysentery, had killed far more soldiers during the war than bullets had. Watery areas where the mosquitoes bred were sprayed with chemicals, helping to stop the spread of the disease. As with many advances in medicine, it came about only after many thousands of soldiers had suffered and died.

THE PRESS AND THE WAR

Without a doubt, the American press—or at least some elements of it—helped provoke America's war with Spain. From 1895, when the revolt in Cuba began, until 1898, when the United States declared war on Spain, the New York *Journal,* owned by William Randolph Hearst, and the New York *World,* owned by Joseph Pulitzer, published stories and editorials that exaggerated accounts of Spanish brutality. Some of the reporters were writing all of this from New York—they were not even in Cuba. Their articles were designed to stir public opinion in favor of military intervention. Hearst and Pulitzer were also fighting one another for advertising dollars, so each paper tried to outsell the other. The sensationalistic reporting came to be known as yellow journalism. Some newspapers followed their lead, while other journalists dismissed their tactics. In the end, yellow journalism triumphed, and the United States went to war with Spain.

Joseph Pulitzer and William Randolph Hearst, the two most powerful newspapermen of the day, are each dressed as the era's most popular cartoon character in "The Big Type War of the Yellow Kids." In their competition to sell papers, Pulitzer and Hearst printed sensational and sometimes completely made-up stories about the Spaniards' treatment of Cubans.

▶ Spanish Atrocities

When General Valeriano Weyler of Spain was sent to Cuba to put down the rebellion, papers such as the New York *Journal* sent correspondents to the island to report on his activities. They accused Weyler of such monstrous atrocities—they nick-named him "Butcher"—that he soon ordered them to leave. But their stories continued, probably based on faulty conclusions and rumor. Some were even faked. Here is a typical atrocity story by James Creelman of the New York *World:*

No man's life, no man's property is safe. American citizens are imprisoned or slain without cause. American property is destroyed on all sides. There is no pretense at protecting it. . . . Millions and millions of dollars worth of American sugar cane, buildings and machinery have already been lost. This year alone the war will strike $68,000,000 from the commerce of the U.S. . . . Wounded soldiers can be found begging in the streets of Havana. . . . Cuba will soon be a wilderness of blackened ruins. This year there is little to live upon. Next year there will be nothing. The horrors of a barbarous struggle for the extermination of the native population are witnessed in all parts of the country. Blood on the roadsides, blood in the fields, blood on the doorsteps, blood, blood, blood! The old, the young, the weak, the crippled—all are butchered without mercy. . . .[1]

Some stories were more specifically aimed at Weyler himself:

If it were possible General Weyler would suppress all newspapers. He hates news. It interferes with his plans to see their execution faithfully reported in the newspapers even before he has had time to receive his official advices. Besides, it must disgust him to read in the press of the cries and groans of the wounded, of the splashing of blood, the heart rending shrieks of the widows and orphans, and all the other incidents of those fusillades by which Spanish authority maintains itself. It must not be supposed that General Weyler is a monster. He is merely a barbarian living in a civilized century. A few hundred years ago our own ancestors chopped their fallen enemies out of their armor plate with

Crucible Of Empire : The Spanish-American War - PBS Online - Microsoft Internet Explorer

File   Edit   View   Favorites   Tools   Help

Address http://www.pbs.org/crucible/frames/_journalism.html   Go

CRUCIBLE of EMPIRE   The Spanish-American War   PBS

YELLOW JOURNALISM

◄ HOME
RELATED LINKS ▼

Hearst Biography
Davis Biography
Headline Gallery
Cartoon Gallery

"Proceed at once to the Philippine Islands. Commence operations

The Spanish-American War is often referred to as the first "media war." During the 1890s, journalism that sensationalized—and sometimes even manufactured—dramatic events was a powerful force that helped propel the United States into war with Spain. Led by newspaper owners William Randolph Hearst and Joseph Pulitzer, journalism of the 1890s used melodrama, romance, and hyperbole to sell

WILLIAM RANDOLPH HEARST

THE FILM

TIMELINE

YELLOW JOURNALISM

1890s MUSIC

RESOURCES

VISITORS'

The PBS Web site *Crucible of Empire: The Spanish-American War* examines the history of yellow journalism and its connection to the war. One of its most famous proponents, William Randolph Hearst, is pictured.

EDITOR'S CHOICE

axes and decapitated them if they could not pay ransom. A few centuries earlier, they used their skulls for drinking cups. But that was not monstrous or unnatural. It was merely barbaric and General Weyler is merely barbaric.[2]

The yellow press of New York was echoed throughout the country. In Indiana, the Frankfort *Times* declared: "Horrors await the Cubans. . . . Weyler will bring total war to the island . . . public executions and torture await the insurgents."[3]

Demands for Intervention

How long would it be, asked the New York *World,* before the United States would help the beleaguered Cubans?

How long are the Spaniards to drench Cuba with the blood and tears of her people?

How long is the peasantry of Spain to be drafted away to Cuba to die miserably in a hopeless war, that Spanish nobles and Spanish officers may get medals and honors?

How long shall old men and women and children be murdered by the score, the innocent victims of Spanish rage against the patriot armies they can not conquer?

How long shall Cuban women be the victims of Spanish outrages and lie sobbing and bruised in loathsome prisons?

How long shall women passengers on vessels flying the American flag be unlawfully seized and stripped and searched by brutal, jeering Spanish officers, in violation of the laws of nations and of the honor of the United States?

How long shall American citizens, arbitrarily arrested while on peaceful and legitimate errands, be immured [enclosed] in foul Spanish prisons without trial?

How long shall the navy of the United States be used as the sea police of barbarous Spain?

How long shall the United States sit idle and indifferent within sound and hearing of rapine [looting] and murder?

How long?[4]

Equally sensational stories appeared in the New York *Journal:*

The experiences of Senora Rodriguez, as related by [this] unfortunate [woman] to the Journal, ought to make every American's blood boil with righteous indignation.

Senora Rodriguez was arrested because her husband was an officer in the Cuban army, locked up in a felon's cell, held incommunicado for three weeks with four other refined women and a company of blaspheming and degraded criminals, taken to Nuevitas in a box car, and thence by steamer to Havana, where she was confined in the House of Refuge for abandoned women, in eleven cells altogether; and after enduring all kinds of insults and privations, was finally sent to Key West through the offices of Consul-General Lee.

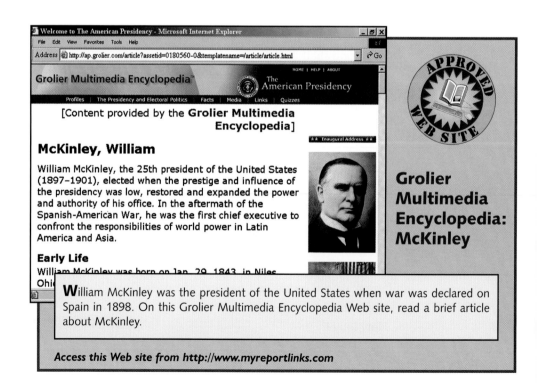

Welcome to The American Presidency - Microsoft Internet Explorer

File Edit View Favorites Tools Help

Address http://ap.grolier.com/article?assetid=0180560-0&templatename=/article/article.html Go

HOME | HELP | ABOUT

Grolier Multimedia Encyclopedia®

The **American Presidency**

Profiles | The Presidency and Electoral Politics | Facts | Media | Links | Quizzes

[Content provided by the **Grolier Multimedia Encyclopedia**]

★★ Inaugural Address ★★

McKinley, William

William McKinley, the 25th president of the United States (1897–1901), elected when the prestige and influence of the presidency was low, restored and expanded the power and authority of his office. In the aftermath of the Spanish-American War, he was the first chief executive to confront the responsibilities of world power in Latin America and Asia.

Early Life

William McKinley was born on Jan. 29, 1843, in Niles, Ohio.

Grolier Multimedia Encyclopedia: McKinley

William McKinley was the president of the United States when war was declared on Spain in 1898. On this Grolier Multimedia Encyclopedia Web site, read a brief article about McKinley.

Access this Web site from http://www.myreportlinks.com

[Fitzhugh Lee was the American representative in Cuba.][5]

Criticizing the Government

President Grover Cleveland opposed intervention and declared that the revolution in Cuba was technically not a war. The press attacked him for this. While atrocities continued, complained the Chicago *Tribune* in 1896, the president did nothing:

Meanwhile a cowardly American president and a cold-blooded American secretary of state [Richard Olney] sit calmly by and declare there is not a state of war in that unfortunate island which has been harried and devastated by war nearly two years. It is not only war, but uncivilized, barbarous, bloody war. It must stop. If the present administration will not stop it the next administration will take the responsibility of stopping it and will thereby earn the plaudits of all humane, civilized, patriotic, liberty-loving Americans.[6]

Popular magazines also joined in the chorus. One of the most widely read magazines of the day was *Leslie's Weekly*. One of its articles in 1896 demanded action by Congress.

As it seems to us, Congress should at once give expression to the feeling of the country as to the savagery which the Spanish commander has introduced into his campaign, and if a dignified remonstrance [plea] in the name of humanity fails to produce any effect, then a stronger argument may properly be resorted to in acknowledgment of the belligerency of the insurgents. . . .[7]

Before the end of 1896, newspapers all over the country campaigned for a formal recognition of Cuban independence. The New York *Journal* not only favored Cuban independence but was already calling for war:

If we are going to give Spain what she chooses to consider a *casus belli* [cause of war], the time to do it is now. She is steadily preparing for such a crisis. Her purchases of ironclads [ships] are manifestly directed against the U.S. She does not need them for the

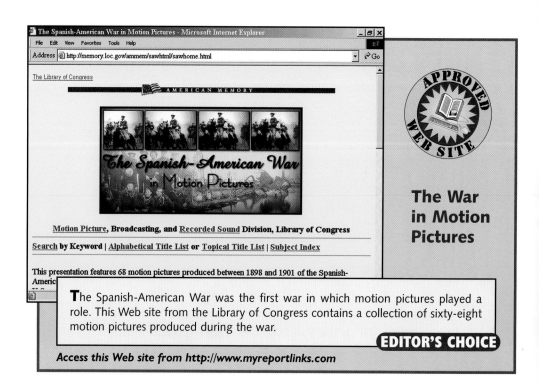

The War in Motion Pictures

The Spanish-American War was the first war in which motion pictures played a role. This Web site from the Library of Congress contains a collection of sixty-eight motion pictures produced during the war.

EDITOR'S CHOICE

Access this Web site from http://www.myreportlinks.com

insurgents, who have neither navy nor fortifications. As yet we have a decisive naval superiority over her, but we are building our own ships, and it takes longer to build them than to buy them. If we intend to intervene for the liberation of Cuba, as a blind man can see we do, not later than next March, and probably not later than December, our obvious policy is to say to Spain, without another day's delay: "This anarchy in Cuba must stop—What do you propose to do about it?"[8]

The Madison, Indiana, *Courier* agreed at least on the question of recognition: "Congress must act to recognize the belligerency on the Cuban people. It is the only honorable course of action."[9]

De Lôme Letter

After becoming president in March 1897, William McKinley followed a cautious policy for about a year. Then early in 1898 came the De Lôme letter and the sinking of the USS *Maine*. The New York *World* published this editorial about the letter's author, Enrique Dupuy de Lôme, the Spanish minister to the United States.

He [De Lôme] has been guilty of an act outrageous and insulting to the country in any case, and peculiarly outrageous and insulting at a time when relations between the two countries are strained almost to the breaking point.

There will be a "disavowal" by the Madrid government, of course. That is polite diplomatic lingo for lying. It ought not to suffice. Until Dupuy De Lôme is punished and assurances are given that his successor

▲ *The wreck of the USS Maine. Two hundred sixty-six men were killed as the result of an explosion aboard the American battleship in Havana Harbor on February 15, 1898.*

will behave like a gentleman, we should receive no successor to him. We at least can get on without any Spanish Minister at Washington.[10]

Destruction of the USS *Maine*

The *World*'s editor was even more forceful in his reaction to the sinking of the USS *Maine*.

Regardless of the question of Cuban independence, unless it be the crowning reason for interference, the destruction of the *Maine* by foul play should be the occasion of ordering our fleet to Havana and demanding proper amends within forty-eight hours under threat of bombardment. If Spain will not punish her miscreants [criminals], we must punish Spain. In brief, the *Maine* was deliberately destroyed by means carefully prepared in advance which means were under absolute control of the Spanish authorities. Spain's responsibility is complete. Yet, as the ambassador has said, "Spain has stood mute and like a wolf takes the consequences of the villainy of her cub!" But was it the cub?[11]

At first, some newspapers urged caution. Said the Indianapolis *Sentinel:* "We must wait . . . It could be [the] result of human error, not treachery."[12]

Others were less cautious. The Columbus, Indiana, *Daily Herald* declared, "There has been too much shuffling diplomacy and lenient action on the part of the United States toward Spain. . . . If it should appear that the destruction of the *Maine* was

The New York Journal and the World, competing newspapers, reached the same conclusion, despite a lack of evidence, after the Maine exploded—that the ship had been mined or torpedoed by the Spaniards. The Journal's headline of February 17, just two days after the ship sank, is blunt in its accusation.

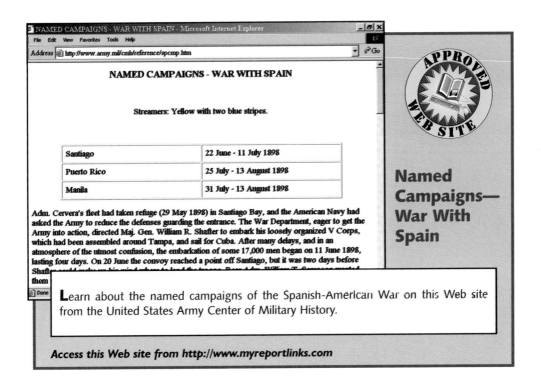

NAMED CAMPAIGNS - WAR WITH SPAIN - Microsoft Internet Explorer

File Edit View Favorites Tools Help

Address http://www.army.mil/cmh/reference/spcmp.htm

NAMED CAMPAIGNS - WAR WITH SPAIN

Streamers: Yellow with two blue stripes.

Santiago	22 June - 11 July 1898
Puerto Rico	25 July - 13 August 1898
Manila	31 July - 13 August 1898

Adm. Cervera's fleet had taken refuge (29 May 1898) in Santiago Bay, and the American Navy had asked the Army to reduce the defenses guarding the entrance. The War Department, eager to get the Army into action, directed Maj. Gen. William R. Shafter to embark his loosely organized V Corps, which had been assembled around Tampa, and sail for Cuba. After many delays, and in an atmosphere of the utmost confusion, the embarkation of some 17,000 men began on 11 June 1898, lasting four days. On 20 June the convoy reached a point off Santiago, but it was two days before Shafter...

Named Campaigns—War With Spain

Learn about the named campaigns of the Spanish-American War on this Web site from the United States Army Center of Military History.

Access this Web site from http://www.myreportlinks.com

▷ Santiago Bay

This battle was a great victory for the Americans, and it essentially ended the war. Under orders to fight, Admiral Cervera led his little squadron out on the open sea at 9:30 in the morning on Sunday, July 3. Henry B. Chamberlin of the New York *Evening Post* described the spectacle:

Into the open sea, their big guns playing under the turtle-backed turrets, rushed the *María Teresa, Colon, Vizcaya,* and *Oquendo.* Coming to meet them . . . were the *Brooklyn, Oregon, Iowa, Texas,* and *Indiana.* . . . Four great battleships began to rain a terrible tonnage of twelve- and thirteen-inch shells, the eight-inch ammunition of the *Brooklyn* shrieked and wailed and howled as it flew on its awful course of destruction, and the starboard side of Commodore Schley's flagship was a continuous line of flame as secondary batteries and rapid-fire guns spit their murderous contents with such terrible rapidity that the heavy smoke from the frightful broadsides seemed to be burned up in the dreadful volume of fire as though it was the purpose to consume the smoke in order that its density might not interfere with the precision of their aim.[19]

Within two hours, this battle was over.

Puerto Rico and the Philippines

In Puerto Rico, there were no great adventures to be described by the correspondents, but in the Philippines there occurred one of the most bizarre developments of the conflict: the staged surrender of Manila. John T. McCutcheon of the Chicago *Record* described that event: "There probably was never a case in history before where two opposing forces combined on the overthrow of one to make a common defense against the third."[20]

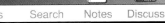

THE WAR IN SONG, POETRY, AND POPULAR LITERATURE

The Spanish-American War was popular with the American people. Most believed it was a marvelous, unselfish undertaking to free the Cuban people from the long oppression of the Spaniards. This feeling, and the desire to avenge the battleship *Maine,* were reflected in the many songs and poems written in 1898. A good example is to be found in the lyrics of "Awake! United States." The first, second, third, and final verses follow.

> *How proudly sailed the warship Maine,*
> *A nation's pride, without a stain!*
> *A wreck she lies, her sailors slain*
> *By treach'rous butchers, paid by Spain!*
>
> *Why does the breeze such sad thoughts bring,*
> *Like murm'ring seas the echoes sing?*
> *Why do the clouds thus backward roll.*
> *Like wave on wave, on rock on shoal!*
>
> *Awake! Thy Stars and Strips unfurl,*
> *And shot and shell and vengeance hurl!*
> *Though clouds may gather, they will go,*
> *And sunlight follow after woe.*

AWAKE UNITED STATES

WORDS & MUSIC BY

MARIE ELIZABETH LAMB.

Published by the

L. GRUNEWALD CO. LT'D.
NEW ORLEANS LA.

Not many suns shall rise and set
Before in battle we have met,
And made the Spanish butchers reel
And downed the banners of Castile![1]

The *Maine* is also remembered in the lyrics of "The *Maine* Goes Fighting On." The first phrase, *Cuba Libre,* is Spanish for "Free Cuba."

"Cuba Libre!" Hear our daughter o're the
            waters stoutly cry,
While the smile that never falters
            from her alters stains the sky,
While the starving men and women
            and the children bravely die—
Yet the Maine goes fighting on!

"Cuba Libre!" Hear the mountains echo
            back the patriot boast!
"Cuba Libre!" Sing the waves along,
            two thousand miles of coast!
"Cuba Libre!" We are coming, it is
            freedom's mighty host
The Maine goes fighting on!

Our gallant sailor martyrs left
            to us the scourging rod.
They are sleeping 'neath the water,
            they are sleeping 'neath the sod.
But their spirits float like lilies
            on the azure seas of God,
The Maine goes fighting on!

Valiant daughters, o're the water,
            we have heard thy many voices,
And the glory of the story makes a patriot
            land rejoice.

Photograph of Evangelina Cisneros - Microsoft Internet Explorer

File Edit View Favorites Tools Help

Address http://www.nypl.org/research/chss/epo/spanexhib/IMAGE-evangelina_cisnero.html

A War in Perspective, 1898–1998, an exhibit of the New York Public Library, focuses on the role of the press during the Spanish-American War. A campaign by Hearst's papers helped free Evangelina Cisneros, a Cuban woman who had been imprisoned in Havana.

> We have wrapped our stars about them,
>   and our swords have made their choice,
> The Maine goes fighting on.[2]

Many songs proclaimed the dedication of Americans to Cuba's fight for independence. The lyrics to "Cuba Must Be Free" declare America's support for the island's fight for freedom.

> 'Tis ours to take up Cuba's plea,
> 'Tis ours to snap the tyrant's chain,

'Tis ours to make the Cubans free,
'Tis ours to break the yoke of Spain.[3]

In "We Are Coming with Old Glory," the Cubans were promised they would soon be free of "the tyranny of Spain."

We have heard you, Cuba, heard you,
And your cry is not in vain;
We are coming now to free you
From the tyranny of Spain!
We are coming!
We are coming!
We are coming with Old Glory
To o're turn the rule of Spain.[4]

No matter how glorious the cause, lives are lost in war. "Freedom for Cuba" acknowledged the sacrifice but declared it would not be in vain.

We will rally at the call boys,
And Cuba shall be free.
Shouting the battle cry, "Free Cuba!"
Though it cost our life and blood
We will give her liberty,
Shouting the battle cry, "Free Cuba!"[5]

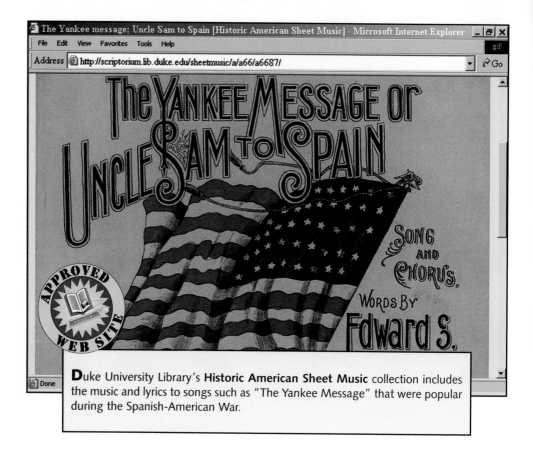

Duke University Library's **Historic American Sheet Music** collection includes the music and lyrics to songs such as "The Yankee Message" that were popular during the Spanish-American War.

In "The Yankee Message," or "Uncle Sam to Spain," the threat of American vengeance and might is made abundantly clear:

I hear across the waters,
From out the southern sea,
The wail of sons and daughters,
In woeful misery,

If you must act the butcher
And helpless ones must die,
I swear by the Eternal,
I'll smite you hip and thigh!

We've got the boys to do it,
A million men and more;
We've got our new-born navy,
And Deweys by the score.

We'll smash your grim old Morros,
And bring them round your ears,
And make the measure honest,
With a thousand "Volunteers."

We greet you gallant Cubans,
We're fighting side by side;
Not yet, O fair Antilles,
Hath sleeping Freedom died;

We'll make that horde "walk Spanish,"
(You hear my thund'rous voice,)
And as between two evils,
We'll give you "Hobson's choice."

Our tears for the dead heroes,
The Maine and martyred crew;
A sigh for smitten sailors,
Who died as patriots do;

But sure as dawns the morrow,
And sure as sets the sun,
We'll avenge our murdered brothers,
Avenge them ev'ry one![6]

Poetry

Admiral George Dewey was one of the great heroes of the war with Spain. He was honored by the American people, the United States government, and the authors and poets of the day. "Our Hero" is a poem that celebrates Dewey's naval victories in the

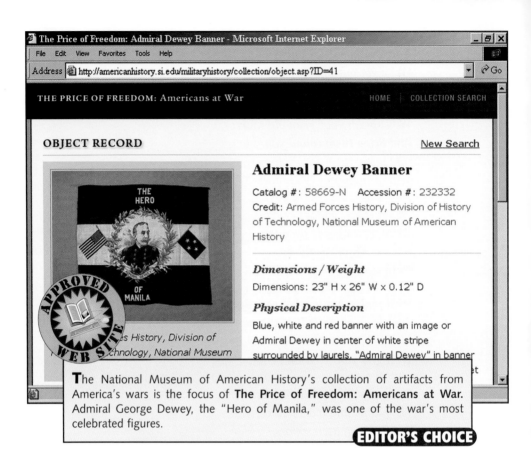

The Price of Freedom: Admiral Dewey Banner - Microsoft Internet Explorer

File Edit View Favorites Tools Help

Address http://americanhistory.si.edu/militaryhistory/collection/object.asp?ID=41

THE PRICE OF FREEDOM: Americans at War   HOME   COLLECTION SEARCH

OBJECT RECORD   New Search

Admiral Dewey Banner

Catalog #: 58669-N   Accession #: 232332
Credit: Armed Forces History, Division of History
of Technology, National Museum of American
History

Dimensions / Weight
Dimensions: 23" H x 26" W x 0.12" D

Physical Description
Blue, white and red banner with an image or
Admiral Dewey in center of white stripe
surrounded by laurels. "Admiral Dewey" in banner

The National Museum of American History's collection of artifacts from America's wars is the focus of **The Price of Freedom: Americans at War.** Admiral George Dewey, the "Hero of Manila," was one of the war's most celebrated figures.

EDITOR'S CHOICE

context of earlier naval heroes such as Hull, Perry, and Decatur, whose exploits in the War of 1812 had become legendary.

Dewey, Dewey, Dewey!
　　　Is the hero of the day.
And the *Maine* has been remembered
　　　In the good, old-fashioned way—
The way of Hull and Perry,
　　　Decatur and the rest—
When old Europe felt the clutches
　　　Of the Eagle of the West;

That's how Dewey smashed the
    Spaniard
In Manila's crooked bay,
        And the Maine has been remembered
In the good, old-fashioned way.[7]

Major General Joseph Wheeler was another hero of the war. An ex-Confederate soldier and a member of Congress, "Fighting Joe" was sixty-two when he volunteered for the Spanish-American War and was given the command of a cavalry division. In this poem by James Lindsay Gordon that appeared in the New York *Tribune,* Wheeler is celebrated for an act of unselfishness in Cuba. Sick with yellow fever, he was riding to the front in an ambulance when he saw wounded soldiers being carried on stretchers. He gave up his place in the ambulance for them and rode the rest of the way on horseback, to the cheers of his men.

General Wheeler At Santiago

Into the thick of the fight he went, pallid and sick and wan,
Borne in an ambulance to the front, a ghostly wisp of a man;
But the fighting soul of a fighting man, approved in the
        long ago,
Went to the front in that ambulance and the body of
        Fighting Joe.

Out from the front they were coming back, smitten of
        Spanish shells—
Wounded boys from the Vermont hills and the Alabama dells;
"Put them into this ambulance; I'll ride to the front," he said:
And he climbed to the saddle and rode right on, that little
        old ex-Confed.

Wheeler - Microsoft Internet Explorer

File   Edit   View   Favorites   Tools   Help

Address 🗋 http://www.spanamwar.com/wheeler.htm   🖉 Go

(left) and General Wheeler (right) inspect a military hospital on Montauk Point

In the American War General Wheeler served as the major general of volunteers
and d   of
San J   n

Done

General Joseph Wheeler, pictured with President William McKinley on **The Spanish-American War Centennial Web Site,** was another hero of the war, celebrated in the press as well as in song.

EDITOR'S CHOICE

From end to end of the long blue ranks rose up the ringing
   cheers,
And many a powder-blackened face furrowed with sodden
   tears,
As with flashing eyes and gleaming sword, and hair and
   beard of snow,
Into the hell of shot and shell rode little old Fighting Joe!

Sick with fever and racked with pain, he could not stay
   away,
For he heard the song of yester-years in the deep-mouthed
   cannon's bay—
He heard in the calling song of the guns there was work for
   him to do,
Where his country's best blood splashed and flowed 'round
   the old Red, White and Blue.

Fevered body and hero heart! This Union's heart to you
Beats cut in love and reverence—and to each dear boy
    in blue
Who stood or fell mid the shot and shell, and cheered in
    the face of the foe,
As, wan and white, to the heart of the fight rode little old
    Fighting Joe![8]

    There were other heroes who did not receive as much publicity but whose courage was captured in poetry. Among them were the African-American troops of the Tenth Cavalry. Their valor at Las

Some of our brave colored Boys who helped to free Cuba.
Copyright 1899 by J. F. Jarvis

Credit: Library of Congress

The Presidio of San Francisco: Buffalo Soldiers is a National Park Service Web page that examines the role that African-American soldiers, sometimes called Buffalo soldiers, played during the Spanish-American War. Some of those soldiers were garrisoned at the Presidio, a fort that is now part of the Golden Gate National Recreation Area.

Guasimas was celebrated in this poem by B. M. Channing:

The Negro Soldier

We used to think the Negro didn't count for very
    much –
Light fingered in the melon patch and chicken yard,
    and such;
Much mixed in point of morals and absurd in point of
    dress,
The butt of droll cartoonists and the target of the press;
But we've got to reconstruct our views on color, more
    or less,
     Now, we know about the Tenth at Las Guasimas!

When a rain of shot was falling, with a song upon his
    lips,
In the horror where such gallant lives went out in
    death's eclipse.
Face to face with Spanish bullets, on the slope of San
    Juan,
The negro soldier showed himself another type of man;
Read the story of his courage coldly, carelessly, who
    can –
     The story of the Tenth at Las Guasimas!

We have heaped the Cuban soil above their bodies,
    black and white –
The strangely sorted comrades of that grand and
    glorious fight –
And many a fair-skinned volunteer goes whole and
    sound to-day
For the succor of the colored troops, the battle records
    say,
And the feud is done forever, of the blue coat and the
    gray –
     All honor to the Tenth at Las Guasimas![9]

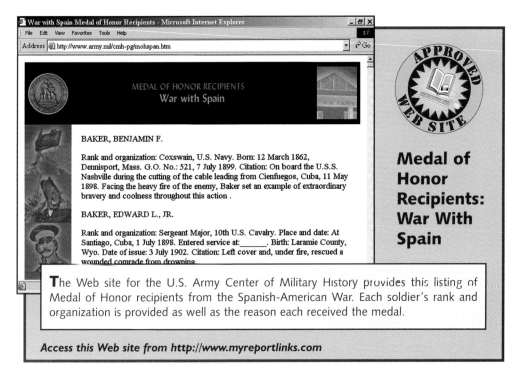

The Web site for the U.S. Army Center of Military History provides this listing of Medal of Honor recipients from the Spanish-American War. Each soldier's rank and organization is provided as well as the reason each received the medal.

Access this Web site from http://www.myreportlinks.com

▶ Books

Many books written during the time of the Spanish-American War echoed the determination of the American people to avenge the *Maine* and free the Cubans. In Edward Stratemeyer's novel *Young Volunteers in Cuba,* the hero, Ben Russell, says: "We owe it to the Cubans and to the cause of humanity to expel the Spanish from Cuba. The poor fellows down there have been fighting for their freedom for three years, and they deserve to have it." Russell also refers to the power of the press at the time when he says, "I've been reading up on this war trouble every day, and I'm going to help the Cubans to freedom and help give Spain the thrashing she deserves."[10]

The popularity of the war was based on the assumption that it was a fight for Cuban independence. That assumption proved incorrect, however, because the United States controlled Cuba for many years afterward. Although that decision was justified as America's best way to protect its interests in the Caribbean, it was made to appear that it was for the Cubans' own good. American leaders claimed that as soon as the Cubans demonstrated that they could actually govern themselves, American control would be lifted. That finally happened in 1929.

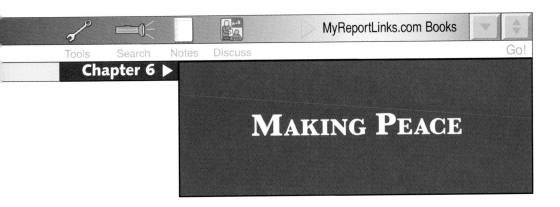

MAKING PEACE

Representatives of the United States and Spain met in Paris from October 1 to December 10, 1898, to negotiate a peace treaty. As far as the Americans were concerned, the only major question was whether or not the United States was going to take possession of all or only part of the Philippines. President McKinley was hesitant, but he concluded that annexation was the only rational course. In one of his speeches, he declared: "We have good money, we have ample revenues, we have unquestioned national credit, but we want new markets, and as trade follows the flag, it looks very much as if we are going to have new markets."[1]

The commissioners that McKinley chose to go to Paris were a distinguished group. The leader was Secretary of State William Day. The others were Whitelaw Reid, publisher of the New York *Tribune,* and Senators Cushman K. Gray of Minnesota, William P. Frye of Maine, and George Gray of Delaware. Reid was the member of the group most in favor of expansion, as his diary shows.

Newspaper editor Whitelaw Reid was rewarded for his support of William McKinley by being named to the Peace Commission following the Spanish-American War.

I believed also that the commerce of the Philippines
. . . with the United States would be very considerable.
Our possession of them would give us an enormous
advantage in the vastly greater commerce that might
be cultivated with China. I believed their possession
valuable to the whole country, but especially important to the Pacific coast. [If] we . . . now added the
Philippines, it would be possible for American energy
to build up such a commercial marine . . . as should
ultimately convert the Pacific Ocean into an American
lake. . . .[2]

Territorial Expansion

When the American commissioners told the Spanish
representatives that the United States intended to
keep the Philippines, the Spaniards were upset but
could do nothing about it. However, the Americans
knew that they had not conquered the Philippines,
so after a time they agreed to pay Spain $20 million.
The Spanish government reluctantly agreed. Other
provisions of the treaty called for the Americans to
retain control of Puerto Rico and Guam and for the
Spaniards to formally give up control of Cuba.
Although Cuba was now theoretically free, the
island remained under the control of the United
States until the American government decided that
Cubans were able to govern themselves.

▷ The Platt Amendment

Cuba was largely controlled by the United States through the terms of a document known as the Platt Amendment, named for Senator Orville Platt of Connecticut. The terms of the amendment gave the United States wide-ranging power over the island as well as the right to establish military bases there. Platt introduced the amendment so that it could be added to a bill appropriating funds for the Army in 1901. Although Cuba officially became an independent republic in 1902, it was forced to incorporate the terms of the Platt Amendment into its own constitution. The United States was involved in Cuba's affairs for thirty-three years. What follows are the important articles of the amendment:

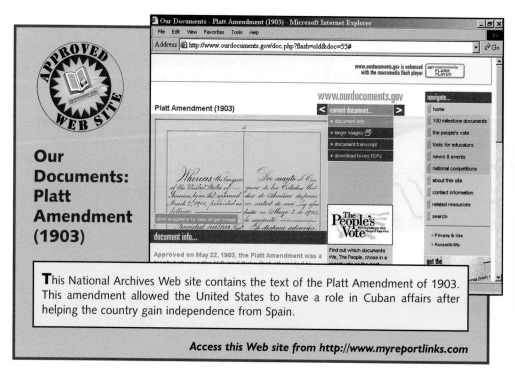

Our Documents: Platt Amendment (1903)

This National Archives Web site contains the text of the Platt Amendment of 1903. This amendment allowed the United States to have a role in Cuban affairs after helping the country gain independence from Spain.

Access this Web site from http://www.myreportlinks.com

Article I. The Government of Cuba shall never enter into any treaty or other compact with any foreign power or powers which will impair or tend to impair the independence of Cuba, nor in any manner authorize or permit any foreign power or powers to obtain by colonization or for military or naval purposes, or otherwise, lodgment in or control over any portion of said island.

Article II. The Government of Cuba shall not assume or contract any public debt to pay the interest upon which, and to make reasonable sinking-fund provision for the ultimate discharge of which, the ordinary revenues of the Island of Cuba, after defraying the current expenses of the Government, shall be inadequate.

Article III. The Government of Cuba consents that the United States may exercise the right to intervene for the preservation of Cuban independence, the maintenance of a government adequate for the protection of life, property, and individual liberty, and for discharging the obligations with respect to Cuba imposed by the Treaty of Paris on the United States, now to be assumed and undertaken by the Government of Cuba . . .

Article V. The Government of Cuba will execute, and as far as necessary, extend the plans already devised, or other plans to be mutually agreed upon, for the sanitation of the cities of the island, to the end that a recurrence of epidemic and infectious diseases may be prevented, thereby assuring protection to the people and commerce of Cuba, as well as to the commerce of the Southern ports of the United States and the people residing therein . . .

Article VII. To enable the United States to maintain the independence of Cuba, and to protect the people thereof, as well as for its own defense, the Government of Cuba will sell or lease to the United States lands necessary for coaling or naval stations, at certain specified points, to be agreed upon with the President of the United States.[3]

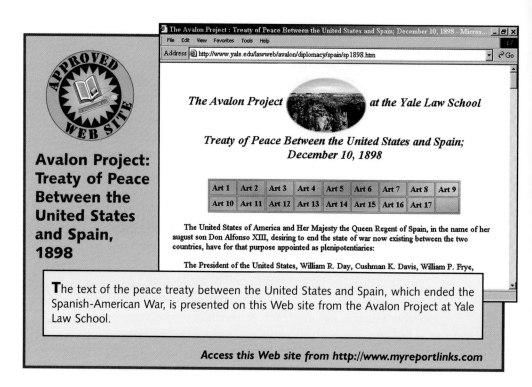

The Avalon Project : Treaty of Peace Between the United States and Spain; December 10, 1898 - Micros...

File Edit View Favorites Tools Help

Address http://www.yale.edu/lawweb/avalon/diplomacy/spain/sp1898.htm

The Avalon Project   *at the Yale Law School*

Treaty of Peace Between the United States and Spain;
December 10, 1898

| Art 1 | Art 2 | Art 3 | Art 4 | Art 5 | Art 6 | Art 7 | Art 8 | Art 9 |
| Art 10 | Art 11 | Art 12 | Art 13 | Art 14 | Art 15 | Art 16 | Art 17 | |

The United States of America and Her Majesty the Queen Regent of Spain, in the name of her august son Don Alfonso XIII, desiring to end the state of war now existing between the two countries, have for that purpose appointed as plenipotentiaries:

The President of the United States, William R. Day, Cushman K. Davis, William P. Frye,

Avalon Project: Treaty of Peace Between the United States and Spain, 1898

The text of the peace treaty between the United States and Spain, which ended the Spanish-American War, is presented on this Web site from the Avalon Project at Yale Law School.

Access this Web site from http://www.myreportlinks.com

▶ Debating the Treaty: Imperialists Versus Anti-Imperialists

The treaty ending the Spanish-American War was signed on December 10, 1898, and was then submitted to the U.S. Senate for ratification. It was finally approved in February 1899, but in the meantime, there was a great debate over it. Many Americans favored the annexation of overseas territories and, for the most part, agreed with the arguments set forth by Whitelaw Reid. Such people were known as imperialists. Those who opposed the treaty, known as anti-imperialists, had many reasons for their opposition. They believed it was wrong for a democracy to impose its will on other people, that overseas expansion was unconstitutional, that overseas possessions would be hard to defend, and that the Philippines would not bring about an economic advantage. Some even believed that because the inhabitants of the new empire were not white, they should not be granted the rights enjoyed by white Americans. Religion also was a factor. Most anti-imperialists were Protestants who did not want the Roman Catholic inhabitants of Cuba or the Philippines to become American citizens.

Many of the anti-imperialist leaders were famous men in influential positions. One of them was Edwin L. Godkin, publisher of *The Nation,* a popular magazine. He listed all that was evil about annexation:

> The sudden departure from our traditions; the absence from our system of any machinery for governing dependencies; the admission of alien, inferior, and mongrel races to our nationality; the opening of fresh fields to . . . speculators, and corruptionists, the un-Americanism of governing a large body of people against their will; . . . the entrance of a policy of conquest and annexation while our own continent was still unreclaimed . . . and many of our most serious political problems unresolved. . . .[4]

Another outspoken anti-imperialist was Andrew Carnegie, a Scottish-born industrialist who helped found America's steel industry and was one of the richest men in the world. When Carnegie received an invitation to a reception honoring the American peace commissioners, he responded sarcastically.

There were influential people who did not approve of America's intervention in the affairs of Cuba and the Philippines. Andrew Carnegie, a Scotsman who immigrated to America, was one of the world's wealthiest men and vehemently opposed to the Spanish-American War.

I shall be in Pittsburgh the evening of your reception to the signers of the WAR treaty with Spain, not the Peace. It is a matter of congratulation however that you seem to have about finished your work of civilizing the Filipinos. It is thought that about 8000 of them have been completely civilized and sent to heaven. I hope you like it.[5]

Another anti-imperialist leader was Senator George F. Hoar of Massachusetts. He campaigned with all his might against annexation and was devastated by his failure. In his autobiography, published in 1904, he sadly concluded:

We crushed the only republic in Asia. We made war on the only Christian people in the East. We converted a war of glory to a war of shame. . . . We inflicted torture on unarmed men to extort confession. We put children to death. . . . We baffled the aspirations of a people for liberty.[6]

Philippine Insurrection

The Filipino revolutionaries, led by Emilio Aguinaldo, were enraged when they realized that the United States did not intend to recognize their independence. At about the same time that the treaty was ratified, war broke out between the revolutionaries and the Americans encamped around Manila. It was an all-out conflict that President McKinley called the

▲ *Early trench warfare: American soldiers fire on Filipino insurgents.*

Philippine Insurrection, but it was really a new phase of the Philippine Revolution. The American commander, General Elwell S. Otis, went on the offensive at once and drove the Filipinos from many of their strongholds in the lowlands into the mountains. Despite these early successes, Otis asked for reinforcements, and McKinley responded by sending several thousand more troops to the islands.

Because it was the objective of American policy to occupy the entire Philippine archipelago, the U.S. Army had to establish bases in many locations. From these bases, American forces moved to engage the enemy and secure control of the main centers of population. Aguinaldo's poorly equipped and trained forces were no match for the Americans. Otis's men, under the field command of Generals Arthur MacArthur and Henry L. Lawton, won victory after victory. By the fall of 1899, the war appeared to be nearly over, but then Aguinaldo changed his strategy. He began to use hit-and-run guerrilla tactics like those used by the rebels in Cuba. He believed that the Americans could not win this type of conflict and would eventually give up.

▲ Although the people of the Philippines had been freed from Spanish rule, they were not free from the American forces who occupied their country. The often brutal warfare between Americans and Filipinos involved the burning of native huts.

▶ Savage Fighting

The second phase of the struggle was fought with great savagery on both sides. There were numerous instances of torture and assassination and the murder of civilians and prisoners. For every act of terror committed by the Filipinos, the Americans responded in kind. In 1900, General Otis was recalled, and General MacArthur was placed in command. MacArthur believed that the only way to end the fighting was to cut the guerrillas off from their sources of supply: the villages. To do this, he established more than five hundred outposts throughout the islands near every important population center. The people in these districts were ordered to move into defined areas that could be defended by the troops stationed nearby. In this way, MacArthur reproduced the concentration policy used by General Weyler in Cuba in 1896—the policy that had driven the United States into war with Spain in the first place. In addition to concentrating civilians in defined areas, MacArthur sent his forces into the field to harass the guerrillas. Now cut off from their sources of supply, the Filipinos could no longer resist effectively, and their military organization collapsed. In 1901, Aguinaldo was captured. Resistance gradually declined after that, and by 1902, the war was finally over.

Chapter 7

FROM CRUSADE TO EMPIRE

The Spanish-American War began as a crusade to free Cuba from Spanish oppression. It ended with the United States acquiring an empire. The American people supported the war at the beginning because they viewed it as a great humanitarian effort, but they also generally supported the final result despite the heated debate over the Treaty of Paris.

▶ The War's Aftermath in the Philippines

The action in the Philippines reflected a change in attitude on the part of American leaders that occurred during the summer of 1898. After Commodore Dewey destroyed the Spanish fleet in Manila Bay, the United States faced a difficult decision. American leaders did not believe that the Filipinos were capable of self-government. They feared that withdrawal would lead to chaos or perhaps intervention by a European power. So they decided to stay. Dr. Jacob Gould Schurman, president of Cornell University, was sent to the Philippines as chairman of a commission to determine whether or not the Filipinos should be left on their own. He concluded:

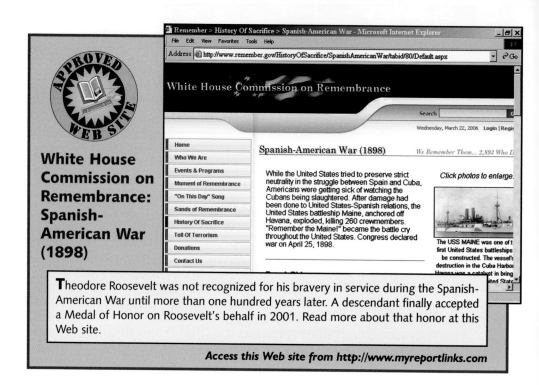

White House Commission on Remembrance: Spanish-American War (1898)

Theodore Roosevelt was not recognized for his bravery in service during the Spanish-American War until more than one hundred years later. A descendant finally accepted a Medal of Honor on Roosevelt's behalf in 2001. Read more about that honor at this Web site.

Access this Web site from http://www.myreportlinks.com

These people with all their racial rivalries would be at each other's throats if we left. And a European power or powers would intervene in a very short time. We must fight to give them good government and educate them gradually for home rule.[1]

American rule in the Philippines began with a military occupation followed by a civilian commission imposed by the United States. In 1902, the Filipinos were allowed to elect a representative assembly. With the Jones Act, passed by Congress in 1916, the United States declared that the Philippines would be granted independence as soon as possible. That finally happened on July 4, 1946.

▷ Cuba and Puerto Rico

The war had long-term consequences in the Caribbean. Even though the Teller Amendment said that Cuba would not be annexed, the Americans concluded that they could not simply withdraw. As in the Philippines, the American government feared that another power might intervene. Most Americans believed that the Cubans, like the Filipinos, could not govern themselves—not only because they lacked experience but also because of high rates of poverty, disease, and illiteracy. So, like the Filipinos, the Cubans found themselves living under military occupation rather than enjoying independence. Many Cubans were angry with the situation, but in the long run, there were benefits. The Americans built roads, established schools, and worked hard to stamp out disease, especially yellow fever.

After the military withdrew, the relationship between the United States and Cuba was governed by the terms of the Platt Amendment. Even though that amendment was abandoned by the United States in 1934, the two countries were linked because American military bases had been established on the island, and American businesses, legal and illegal, flourished there. Then, in 1959, Fidel Castro came to power in Cuba and allied himself with the Soviet Union. Cuba became dependent on Soviet aid and economic support. When the Soviet Union was dismantled in 1989, the Cuban economy also collapsed. Castro remains in power, but Cuba

▲ *The streets of Havana, Cuba, look peaceful in this photograph from 1900. Although Cuba would become an independent republic in 1902, the Platt Amendment and American investments in Cuba kept the United States involved in Cuban affairs until 1959, when Fidel Castro came to power.*

suffers from many problems because its economy is still controlled by Cuba's Socialist government.

Puerto Rico was governed by the United States military from 1898 until 1900. In 1900, Puerto Ricans were allowed a civil government consisting of a governor and a two-house legislature, but the governor was an American, and the members of the upper house of the legislature were appointed, not elected. In 1917, the U.S. Congress passed a law that allowed Puerto Ricans to elect their own government. Since 1952, Puerto Rico has been designated a commonwealth of the United States. The people of Puerto Rico are American citizens. They can immigrate freely, serve in the military, and vote for their own governor and legislature, but they cannot vote for president or members of Congress. The vast majority of Puerto Ricans seem to be satisfied with this arrangement.

America Changed Forever

The birth of the American empire also marked the emergence of the United States as a world power. The nation now had interests in the Caribbean and the Far East and it was hoped that possession of these far-flung territories would open doors to increased trade and business. It did, but the territories would

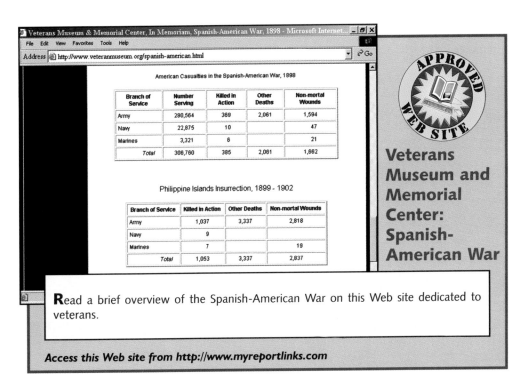

American Casualties in the Spanish-American War, 1898

Branch of Service	Number Serving	Killed in Action	Other Deaths	Non-mortal Wounds
Army	280,564	369	2,061	1,594
Navy	22,875	10		47
Marines	3,321	6		21
Total	306,760	385	2,061	1,662

Philippine Islands Insurrection, 1899 - 1902

Branch of Service	Killed in Action	Other Deaths	Non-mortal Wounds
Army	1,037	3,337	2,818
Navy	9		
Marines	7		19
Total	1,053	3,337	2,837

Veterans Museum and Memorial Center: Spanish-American War

Read a brief overview of the Spanish-American War on this Web site dedicated to veterans.

Access this Web site from http://www.myreportlinks.com

Thomas Brackett Reed of Maine was the Speaker of the House of Representatives during the Spanish-American War. Reed, who opposed the war and America's imperialist leanings, resigned from Congress in 1899.

also have to be defended, and that necessity changed the relationship of the United States with the rest of the world.

Speaker of the House Thomas B. Reed, a Republican from Maine, spoke of his regret over the change in the United States that had come about as a result of the Spanish-American War.

At the beginning . . . we were most admirably situated. We had no standing army which could overrun our people. We were at peace within our own borders and with all the world. . . . We were then in a condition which secured to us the respect and envy of the civilized world. The quarrels which other nations have we did not have. The sun did set on our dominions and our drum-beat did not encircle the world with our martial airs. Our guns were not likely to be called upon to throw projectiles which cost, each of them, the price of a happy home, nor did any bombardment seem likely to cost us the value of a village.[2]

Report Links

The Internet sites described below can be accessed at http://www.myreportlinks.com

▶**Crucible of Empire: The Spanish-American War**
Editor's Choice This PBS Web site provides extensive coverage of the Spanish-American War.

▶**The World of 1898: The Spanish-American War**
Editor's Choice Learn more about the events and people of the Spanish-American War.

▶**The War in Motion Pictures**
Editor's Choice View a collection of movies of the Spanish-American War.

▶**The Price of Freedom: Americans at War**
Editor's Choice View Spanish-American War artifacts from the National Museum of American History.

▶**Wisconsin War Letters: The Spanish-American War**
Editor's Choice Read letters written by soldiers from Wisconsin who served in the war.

▶**The Spanish-American War Centennial Web Site**
Editor's Choice This site offers a wealth of information about the war and its aftermath.

▶**Avalon Project: Treaty of Peace Between the United States and Spain, 1898**
Read the text of the treaty that brought an end to the Spanish-American War.

▶**Commodore George Dewey**
Read about Commodore George Dewey's role in the Spanish-American War.

▶**The Destruction of USS *Maine***
Learn about the explosion on the USS *Maine* and why it led to war with Spain.

▶**Digitized Primary American History Sources**
View a collection of primary sources of American history.

▶**The Era of William McKinley**
This Web site looks at the era of William McKinley.

▶**Grolier Multimedia Encyclopedia: McKinley**
Read a biography of President William McKinley on this site.

▶**Historic American Sheet Music**
View Duke University's collection of historic sheet music on this site.

▶**Historical Museum of South Florida: The Spanish-American War**
An online exhibit on the Spanish-American War and its effect in Florida is offered.

▶**Illinois Citizen-Soldier: A Look Through Time**
Learn about soldiers from Illinois who served in the Spanish-American War.

Report Links

The Internet sites described below can be accessed at http://www.myreportlinks.com

▶**Medal of Honor Recipients: War With Spain**
Read about those who received the Medal of Honor during the Spanish-American War.

▶**Named Campaigns—War With Spain**
The Army's Center of Military History Web site gives a brief overview of the war's battles.

▶**The National Archives: The Spanish-American War**
View primary source documents from the Spanish-American War.

▶**National Museum of Health & Medicine: Spanish-American War**
Read about the failures and successes treating sick and wounded soldiers during the war.

▶**Our Documents: De Lôme Letter (1898)**
Read the letter that helped gain public support for a war with Spain.

▶**Our Documents: Platt Amendment (1903)**
Read the text of the Platt Amendment, which kept the United States involved in Cuba.

▶**Presidio of San Francisco: Buffalo Soldiers**
Learn about the role of Buffalo soldiers in the Spanish-American War.

▶**Spanish-American War Maps**
Maps showing Spanish-American War campaigns can be found on this West Point Web site.

▶**Spanish-American War Gallery**
The images on this site show Spanish-American War soldiers training in Florida camps.

▶**The Spanish-American War in the Philippines**
Learn about the fight in the Philippines.

▶**Theodore Roosevelt Association**
Learn more about Theodore Roosevelt and the Rough Riders on this Web site.

▶**Theodore Roosevelt: Icon of the American Century**
Explore this National Portrait Gallery exhibit of Theodore Roosevelt.

▶**Veterans Museum and Memorial Center: Spanish-American War**
Read a brief overview of the war on this Web site dedicated to veterans.

▶**A War in Perspective, 1898–1998**
View an exhibit of the Spanish-American War on this New York Public Library site.

▶**White House Commission on Remembrance: Spanish-American War (1898)**
This site explores the saga of Theodore Roosevelt and the Medal of Honor for his war service.

annexation—To make a country or territory part of another country.

anti-imperialist—One who opposes territorial expansion.

Antilles—Cuba and Puerto Rico are part of a group of islands in the West Indies known as the Greater Antilles.

archipelago—A series of islands.

ardor—Intense emotion.

armistice—A break in the fighting of a war to begin talks for peace.

belligerency—A recognition of a state of war involving two or more states.

blockade—A naval maneuver designed to prevent access to the coast of an enemy.

boatswain—A noncommissioned officer on a ship in charge of its maintenance and equipment.

Cabinet—Advisors to the president, including the secretary of state, secretary of war, and others.

casus belli—Latin for "cause of war."

commodore—A naval officer above a captain and below a rear admiral.

dysentery—An infectious disease causing severe diarrhea.

flagship—The ship from which an admiral or another officer directs a fleet.

fusillades—Rapid or simultaneous discharge of many firearms.

galley—The kitchen area on a ship.

guerrilla fighters—Combatants who are not part of a regular army and who fight using hit-and-run tactics.

hardtack—A hard, dry biscuit, bread, or cracker made from water and flour, it was a staple for sailors and soldiers for centuries.

hetacomb—A horrible event.

Hobson's choice—A choice without an alternative.

imperialists—People who favor territorial expansion.

insurgents—People who rise up in rebellion.

insurrection—A revolution or struggle against an oppressive occupier.

ironclads—Naval vessels with sides and decks protected by iron or steel plates.

joint resolution—A vote by both houses of Congress.

Mauser—The standard rifle used by Spanish forces in the Spanish-American War.

military attaché—A person who represents the military of one nation to the military of another nation.

pacification—The process of bringing about peace or stopping hostilities.

peace protocol—An agreement preceding a peace treaty.

plaudits—Approval or thanks.

rabble—An insulting term for people considered insignificant.

ratification—The approval of a legal entity, such as a law or treaty, by the U.S. Senate.

reconcentration—Spain's policy in Cuba in which large groups of Cubans in certain areas were forced to leave their homes and go into concentration camps.

sabotage—The deliberate damaging or destruction of property and/or equipment to undermine an opponent.

septic—One who has sepsis, a toxic spread of bacteria through the bloodstream.

sortie—A military attack by a small force into enemy territory.

succor—Relief or help.

yellow journalism—A term that describes the sensationalist journalists of the era of the Spanish-American War.

Chapter 1. A Hero Is Born: The Battle of Manila Bay, May 1, 1898

1. Joseph L. Stickney, *The Life of Admiral George Dewey and the Conquest of the Philippines* (Philadelphia: P. W. Ziegler and Company, 1899), p. 44.

2. Frank Freidel, *The Splendid Little War* (New York: Bramhold House, 1958), p. 3.

3. Henry F. Pringle, *Theodore Roosevelt, A Biography* (New York: Harcourt, Brace and Company, 1931), p. 178.

4. Freidel, p. 15.

5. Ibid.

6. Ibid., p. 17.

7. Ibid., pp. 23–24.

8. Charles H. Brown, *The Correspondents' War: Journalists in the Spanish-American War* (New York: Scribner's, 1967), p. 195.

9. Stickney, p. 13.

Chapter 2. A Brief History of the War

1. Marcus M. Wilkerson, *Public Opinion and the Spanish-American War* (New York: Russell and Russell, 1932), p. 92.

2. Lawrence Shaw Mayo, *America of Yesterday as Reflected in the Journal of John Davis Long* (Boston: Atlantic Monthly Press, 1935), pp. 161–162.

3. Ibid., pp. 163–164.

4. Congressional Record, 55th Congress, 2nd Session, March 17, 1898, pp. 2916–2919.

5. George J. A. O'Toole, *The Spanish War, An American Epic—1898* (New York: W. W. Norton & Co., 1984), pp. 169–70. With permission of W. W. Norton & Co.

6. *The World of 1898: The Spanish-American War,* Hispanic Division, Library of Congress, n.d., <http://www.loc.gov/rr/hispanic/1898/> (April 25, 2006).

7. Reprinted from *The Little War of Private Post: The Spanish-American War Seen Up Close* by Charles Johnson Post (Lincoln: University of Nebraska Press, 1967), p. 4. Reprinted with permission of University of Nebraska Press.

8. Theodore Roosevelt, *The Rough Riders* (New York: Scribner's, 1926), pp. 1–2.

9. Walter Millis, *The Martial Spirit* (Cambridge: The Riverside Press, 1931), pp. 27–48.

10. George J. A. O'Toole, *The Spanish War, An American Epic—1898* (New York: W. W. Norton & Co., 1984), p. 244. With permission of W. W. Norton & Co.

11. David Trask, *The War With Spain in 1898* (New York: MacMillan, 1981), pp. 63–64.

12. Mayo, p. 202.

13. Frank Freidel, *The Splendid Little War* (New York: Bramhold House, 1958), p. 280.

Chapter 3. Voices of War: The Combatants Speak

1. John Bigelow, Jr., *Reminiscences of the Santiago Campaign* (New York and London: Harper and Brothers, 1899), p. 82.

2. Ibid., pp. 89–90.

3. Maximo Gómez, *Diary of My Campaigns, 1869–1899* (Havana, Cuba: 1940), No pagination. Entry is from June 24, 1898.

4. Frank Freidel, *The Splendid Little War* (New York: Bramhold House, 1958), pp. 133–135.

5. Ibid., p. 138.

6. Ibid., p. 139.

7. Ibid., p. 140.

8. Ibid., p. 158.

9. E. J. McClernand, *Reminiscences of the Santiago Campaign* (Private, 1922), p. 292.

10. Theodore Roosevelt, *The Rough Riders* (New York: Scribner's, 1926), pp. 168–169.

11. Reprinted from *The Little War of Private Post: The Spanish-American War Seen Up Close* by Charles Johnson Post (Lincoln: University of Nebraska Press, 1967), p. 195. Reprinted with permission of University of Nebraska Press.

12. David Trask, *The War With Spain in 1898* (New York: MacMillan, 1981), p. 258.

13. Freidel, p. 193.

14. Ibid., p. 194.

15. Ibid., p. 193.

16. José Muller Tejeria, *Combates y Capitulación de Santiago,* "The Battle and Surrender of Santiago" (Madrid, Spain: 1898), No pagination.

17. Trask, p. 266.

18. Freidel, pp. 255–256.

19. A. Holloway, *Hero Tales of the American Soldier and Sailor* (Philadelphia: Elliott, 1899), pp. 127–128.

20. Gómez, July 23, 1898, No pagination.

21. George G. King, *Letters of a Volunteer in the Spanish-American War* (Chicago: Hawkins and Loomis, 1929), p. 50.

22. Ibid., p. 54.

23. Ibid., p. 133.

24. Freidel, pp. 273, 275.

25. Finley Peter Dunne, *Mr. Dooley in Peace and War* (Champaign-Urbana: University of Illinois Press, 1898), pp. 20–22.

26. Freidel, p. 277.

27. Ibid., p. 279.

28. Ibid., pp. 290–291.

29. Reprinted from *The Little War of Private Post: The Spanish-American War Seen Up Close* by Charles Johnson Post (Lincoln: University of Nebraska Press, 1967), pp. 295–296, 305, 316, 340. Reprinted with permission of University of Nebraska Press.

30. National Museum of Health and Medicine, "Spanish-American War: Surgery and Asepsis," n.d., <http://nmhm.washingtondc.museum/exhibits/past/Span_Am_WAr/surgery/surgery.html> (March 20, 2006).

Chapter 4. The Press and the War

1. New York *World,* May 17, 1896, from Marcus M. Wilkerson, *Public Opinion and the Spanish-American War* (New York: Russell and Russell, 1932), p. 32.

2. New York *World*, May 8, 1896, Wilkerson, pp. 36–37.

3. Frankfort *Times,* January 20, 1896. Quoted in Martin M. Rosenburg, *Indiana and the Coming of the Spanish-American War, Ball State Monograph, No. 26, Publication in History* (No. 4, Muncie, Ind.: Ball State University, 1976), p. 13.

4. New York *World,* February 13, 1897, Wilkerson, pp. 40–41.

5. New York *Journal,* March 2, 1897, Wilkerson, p. 45.

6. Chicago *Tribune,* December 3, 1896, Wilkerson, p. 49.

7. *Leslie's Weekly,* (LXXXII, March 5, 1896), Wilkerson, p. 51.

8. New York *Journal,* September 16, 1896, Wilkerson, p. 74.

9. Madison *Courier,* January 29, 1896, Rosenberg, p. 16.

10. New York *World,* February 10, 1898, Wilkerson, pp. 93–94.

11. New York *World,* April 1, 1898, Wilkerson, pp. 114–115.

12. Indianapolis *Sentinel,* February 17, 1898, Rosenberg, p. 25.

13. Columbus *Daily Herald,* February 20, 1898, Rosenberg, p. 27.

14. Freidel, pp. 113–114.

15. R. W. Stallman and E. R. Hagemann, eds., *The War Dispatches of Stephen Crane* (Westport, Conn.: Greenwood Press, 1964), p. 157.

16. Burr McIntosh, *The Little I Saw of Cuba* (New York: F. Tennyson Neely, 1898), pp. 90–91.

17. Charles H. Brown, *The Correspondents' War: Journalists in the Spanish-American War* (New York: Scribner's, 1967), pp. 344–345.

18. Douglas Allen, *Frederic Remington and the Spanish-American War* (New York: Crown Publishers, 1971), p. 112.

19. Brown, pp. 378, 380.

20. Ibid., p. 427.

Chapter 5. The War in Song, Poetry, and Popular Literature

1. "Awake! United States," words and music by Marie Elizabeth Lamb, published by Grunewald Company, Ltd., 1898, in *Digital Scriptorium,* Rare Book, Manuscript, and Special Collections Library, Duke University, n.d., <http://scriptorium.lib.duke.edu/sheetmusic/search.html> (March 17, 2006).

2. "The Maine Goes Fighting On," written and published by Charles H. Crandall, 1898 (Courtesy of the Stamford Historical Society, Inc., Stamford, Connecticut).

3. Louis A. Pérez, Jr., *The War of 1898: The United States and Cuba in History and Historiography* (Chapel Hill: University of North Carolina Press, 1998), p. 25.

4. Ibid.

5. Ibid.

6. "The Yankee Message, or Uncle Sam to Spain," written and published by Charles M. Hattersley, 1898, in *Digital Scriptorium,* Rare Book, Manuscript, and Special Collections Library, Duke University, n.d., <http://scriptorium.lib.duke.edu/sheetmusic/search.html> (March 17, 2006).

7. Joseph L. Stickney, *The Life of Admiral George Dewey and the Conquest of the Philippines* (Philadelphia: P. W. Ziegler and Company, 1899), pp. 416–418.

8. Hershel V. Cashin et al., *Under Fire with the Tenth U.S. Cavalry* (N.H.: Ayer Company Publishers, 1899), pp. 276–277. With permission of Ayer Company Publishers.

9. Ibid.

10. Pérez, p. 27.

Chapter 6. Making Peace

1. H. Wayne Morgan, *William McKinley and His America* (Syracuse: Syracuse University Press, 1963), p. 407.

2. H. Wayne Morgan, ed., *Making Peace With Spain: The Diary of Whitelaw Reid* (Austin: University of Texas Press, 1968), p. 29.

3. C. I. Blevans, ed., "The Platt Amendment," in *Treaties and Other International Agreements of the United States of America, 1776–1949*, vol. 8 (Washington, D.C.: Government Printing Office, 1971), pp. 1116–1117.

4. Robert L. Beisner, *Twelve Against Empire: The Anti-Imperialists, 1898–1900* (New York: McGraw-Hill, 1968), p. 76.

5. Ibid., p. 175.

6. Ibid., p. 162.

Chapter 7. From Crusade to Empire

1. Jacob Gould Schurman to Mrs. Schurman, April 7, 1899, Schurman Collection, Olin Library, Cornell University, Ithaca, New York, in the Pacific Coast Branch, American Historical Association, *Pacific Historical Review*, vol. xxvi (Berkeley: University of California Press, 1967), p. 409.

2. Robert L. Beisner, *Twelve Against Empire: The Anti-Imperialists, 1898–1900* (New York: McGraw-Hill, 1968), p. 208.

Brannen, Daniel E., Jr. *Spanish-American War.* Detroit: UXL, 2003.

Collier, Christopher, and James Lincoln Collier. *The United States Enters the World Stage: From Alaska Purchase Through World War I, 1867–1919.* New York: Benchmark Books, 2001.

Dolan, Edward F. *The Spanish-American War.* Brookfield, Conn.: Millbrook Press, 2001.

Flanagan, Alice K. *The Buffalo Soldiers.* Minneapolis: Compass Point Books, 2005.

Golay, Michael. *Spanish-American War.* New York: Facts on File, 2003.

Green, Carl R. *The Spanish-American War: A MyReportLinks.com Book.* Berkeley Heights, N.J.: MyReportLinks.com Books, 2002.

Kraft, Betsey Harvey. *Theodore Roosevelt: Champion of the American Spirit.* New York: Clarion Books, 2003.

Langellier, John P. *Uncle Sam's Little Wars: The Spanish-American War, Philippine Insurrection and Boxer Rebellion, 1898–1902.* Philadelphia: Chelsea House Publishers, 2002.

McNeese, Tim. *Remember the Maine!: The Spanish-American War Begins.* Greensboro, N.C.: Morgan Reynolds, 2002.

Santella, Andrew. *Roosevelt's Rough Riders.* Minneapolis: Compass Point Books, 2006.

Scheuler, Donald G. *Theodore Roosevelt: A MyReportLinks.com Book.* Berkeley Heights, N.J.: MyReportLinks.com Books, 2002.

Staten, Clifford L. *The History of Cuba.* Westport, Conn.: Greenwood Press, 2003.

Sullivan, George. *Journalists at Risk: Reporting America's Wars.* Minneapolis: Twenty-First Century Books, 2006.

Wukovits, John F. *The Spanish-American War.* San Diego: Lucent Books, 2002.